**W9-ACE-336**

DISCARDED
JENKS LRC
GORDON COLLEGE

25—
TC27046

# Recalled to Life

*Professor Moshe Goshen-Gottstein (October 1989).*

❖ ❖ ❖ ❖ ❖ ❖ ❖ ❖ ❖ ❖ ❖ ❖ ❖ ❖

# Recalled to Life

## The Story of a Coma

❖ ❖ ❖ ❖ ❖ ❖ ❖ ❖ ❖ ❖ ❖ ❖ ❖ ❖

ESTHER GOSHEN-GOTTSTEIN

with a foreword by Oliver Sacks, M.D.

Yale University Press   New Haven & London

JENKS L.R.C.
GORDON COLLEGE
255 GRAPEVINE RD.
WENHAM, MA 01984-1895

RB
150
.C6
G6713
1990

Published with assistance from the
Louis Stern Memorial Fund.
Copyright © April 1988 by Schocken
Publishing House, Tel-Aviv, Israel.
English-language edition copyright ©
1990 by Yale University.
All rights reserved.
This book may not be reproduced, in
whole or in part, including illustrations,
in any form (beyond that copying
permitted by Sections 107 and 108 of
the U.S. Copyright Law and except by
reviewers for the public press), without
written permission from the publishers.

Designed by Richard Hendel.
Set in Berkeley Book type by
Tseng Information Systems, Durham,
North Carolina.
Printed in the United States of
America by Edwards Brothers, Inc., Ann
Arbor, Michigan.

Library of Congress
Cataloging-in-Publication Data
Goshen-Gottstein, Esther R.
    [Gilui lev. English]
Recalled to life: the story of a coma/
Esther Goshen-Gottstein : with a
foreword by Oliver Sacks.
        p.    cm.
Translation of: Gilui lev.
    Includes bibliographical references.
ISBN 0–300–04473–9 (alk. paper)
1. Goshen-Gottstein, Moshe H. (Moshe
Henry), 1925–    —Health.
2. Coma—Patients—Israel—Biography.
3. Linguists—Israel—Biography. 4.
Aortocoronary bypass— Complications
and sequelae. I. Title.
RB150.C6G6713    1990
362.1'96849—dc20
[B]                    90–33952
                          CIP

The paper in this book meets the
guidelines for permanence and
durability of the Committee on
Production Guidelines for Book
Longevity of the Council on
Library Resources.

10 9 8 7 6 5 4 3 2 1

*To the hero of this book*

*who returned to us*

# Contents

# Foreword

OLIVER SACKS, M.D.

To be thrown into a deep coma, followed by a "vegetative" state, is considered by neurologists a hopeless business—there are no documented cases of recovery from such a state (except, very occasionally, by youthful patients following an acute head injury).

Thus when Professor Goshen-Gottstein, an eminent linguist in his sixtieth year, suffered severe brain damage as a result of complications during a coronary bypass operation (a heart attack and a profound drop in blood pressure had starved his brain of oxygen) no realistic hopes could be entertained for his recovery.

But his wife and family *did* hope, hoped and prayed that the unprecedented, the "miraculous," might occur. Was this wholly unrealistic—absurd? Mrs. Goshen-Gottstein, herself a psychologist, combed the medical literature, which gave absolutely no grounds for hope —but as she extended her questioning, she heard anecdotes of supposedly impossible recoveries, which seemed to give some support to her hopes.

Against all the statistics, against all reasonable expectation, Professor Goshen-Gottstein recovered. He emerged from a coma of many weeks' duration. Then, through the ensuing months—helped by intensive rehabilitative efforts; by the support and resourcefulness of his family, who never lost faith in the possibility of a complete recovery; and, not least, by his own indomitable will, which recalls that of Luria's patient Zazetsky, the hero-victim of *The Man with a Shattered World*—Professor Goshen-Gottstein climbed back through often terrifying disabilities (he had lost much of his recent memory, his orientation in time and space, his sense of number, some of his power of language, his emotional control, and much of the strength and sense of his left side). He finally achieved almost complete neurological and intellectual recovery. Within eighteen months of his "terminal" brain damage, Professor Goshen-Gottstein had written two books and countless scholarly articles, attended conferences, lectured widely, and been appointed to visiting professorships at Harvard and Brandeis Universities.

This, then, is the story of an "impossible" recovery, told with great feeling, but also with great precision and objectivity, by his wife. At the end there is a poignant chapter by Professor Goshen-Gottstein himself. This is the story not only of a man's illness and recovery but of the crucial part a family can and must play in such a drama.

There is a tendency to ignore people in coma—to treat them as "vegetables," as effectively dead. It may be important to speak to the comatose person, to show one's love, to keep him or her informed, even though there is no apparent response. Whether this is mere "auditory stimulation" (for the brainstem's responses to music and sounds are preserved even in deep coma) or whether it calls upon some deeply unconscious but still present person remains unclear. But there is a suggestion, and more than a suggestion, that sometimes speaking to and touching the comatose person may serve to shorten coma.

Certainly Professor Goshen-Gottstein's family and friends were exemplary in this regard. He was provided with rich human stimulation, not left in that state of environmental deprivation which is so often the lot of those in coma. And when Professor Goshen-Gottstein began to return to life—such returns may be fraught with their own mortifying hazards—there was a family presence and a rehabilitative presence which was, above all, *tactful,* calling him to challenge his limits, to realize his potential, without ever pushing him cruelly or heedlessly beyond his capabilities. One sees here, beautifully laid out, the whole structure of recovery, its ethical and social aspects no less than the medical.

Anecdotes of recovery exist, but this is the first fully documented report known to me of a "return" from a deep coma where no return seemed possible. The medical interest of such a case is very great, and it is essential that such cases be written up. One of Professor Goshen-Gottstein's physicians has published a brief account in the medical literature (reprinted as an appendix to this book).

But this book is much more than a mere report of an interesting (or even unique) case. It is an intensely human document of a man's suffering, fortitude, dignity, and recovery, and of the powers of care and faith which did so much to make his final triumph possible. Such experiences carry an affirmation and a lesson for us all, and one must now hope that this remarkable narrative, recently published in Israel to critical praise and popular acclaim, will find the English-speaking audience it deserves.

# Preface

"What made you write this book?" one of my friends recently asked. I was amazed by the question until I realized that it could not be obvious to the uninitiated why I had been almost driven to put my experiences on paper.

I had participated in an event so special, so unique, that I felt it incumbent on me to share it with as many people as possible. Some close friends and relatives were thousands of miles away when these events occurred; I wanted them to know in detail what had happened. At the same time I felt that a broader public might also be moved by the tale of a man who, after being unconscious for almost four months, gradually returned to a full, meaningful, and creative life.

A Hebrew version of this book was published in 1988, entitled *Gilui Lev* (Unfolding of the heart). The present English edition incorporates several additions and changes as well as a foreword by Dr. Oliver Sacks; hence the two books are not identical. The account is a true and accurate one, though many names have been changed.

It gives me great joy to express my indebtedness to Moshe, my husband. This in a sense is really his book.

I also want to express gratitude to the people who have been most crucial in the book's evolution. To Krystyna Kaufman I owe the idea of noting down the signs of improvement in Moshe. It was she who suggested that I could eventually share these notes with Moshe, once he had emerged from his coma. The idea not only instilled hope in me but also served as the basis for this book; without such notes I could not have reconstructed the story in its manifold details.

Professor Moshe Davies gave me the first push toward writing the book by presenting me with a deadline for the first few chapters, so that he could show them to a writer friend in New York on one of his trips to the United States. Dr. Rodney Falk, our friend and neighbor, was returning to Boston at the beginning of 1986—hence I had to get the important medical facts down quickly so that he could correct them if necessary.

An array of people served as unofficial editors at one point or another. Foremost among them are my friends Dr. Bayla Sarfatti-Schorr and Dr. David Noel Freedman, my brother Gershon, and my son Alon. Their criticisms and suggestions were invaluable and enabled me to avoid the grossest blunders. But of course the responsibility for any errors is mine alone.

I drew great strength and pleasure from Dr. Oliver Sacks, who, after reading my manuscript, not only encouraged me to hope for its publication in the United States but also generously agreed to write a foreword to the English version.

I am indebted to Professor Bill Daleski for suggesting the title of the book, which originates from Charles Dickens's *Tale of Two Cities*.

Last but not least, I owe a special debt to my editors: Carmella Eban-Ross, for handling an earlier version of my manuscript with skill and sensitivity, and Gladys Topkis, Senior Editor at Yale University Press, for her enthusiasm about this book. As a superb reader she rendered expert assistance in shaping its final form, ably supported by Stef Jones.

# 1

## Operation

The evening of June 3, 1985, was cool and refreshing after the heat of the day. We had just seen Michael Pennington of London's Royal Shakespeare Company as Anton Chekhov at the Jerusalem Khan Theater. There could have been no more fitting introduction to the medical drama that was about to unfold, although of course I didn't know this at the time.

The trip home usually takes no more than twelve minutes on foot. This time it took forty minutes—Moshe had to stop and inhale deeply every few steps. It was clear to both of us that something was radically wrong.

Moshe, then aged fifty-nine, had for many years experienced back pain during such strenuous physical activity as climbing hills. His doctors had repeatedly assured him that the pain was of orthopedic origin. Moshe, however, was convinced that the doctors were mistaken—he believed his back pain stemmed from cardiac problems.

It was constantly on his mind that both of his parents had died in their sixties following heart attacks. Like them, he was obese (he weighed close to two hundred pounds at the time) and suffered from diabetes mellitus and high blood pressure. A year earlier he had been told that he had angina pectoris, and his doctor had finally agreed that his back pain resulted from insufficient blood supply to the heart, caused by coronary vascular disease.

Rodney, a cardiologist who had recently become our neighbor and friend, was at home when we returned from the theater. He came as soon as I called, examined Moshe, and announced regretfully that he would have to hospitalize Moshe the next morning. On June 4, Moshe was admitted to the intensive coronary unit at the Shaare Zedek Medical Center. The diagnosis was "unstable angina pectoris."

At first the doctors attempted to stabilize Moshe with large amounts of oral medication. To test the efficacy of this treatment they gave him home leave on a Thursday, ten days after he had been admitted to the unit. Moshe used the first hour of his freedom to make a short appearance at the wedding of the daughter of Aliza and Zvi, our friends of long duration. They were overjoyed to see him. When Aliza later gave me a photograph of Moshe that had been taken at the wedding, we all feared that it would be the last picture we would have of him. I could not bear to look at it.

During the following night, Moshe had two severe attacks of anginal pain which completely exhausted him. It was evident that despite large doses of oral medication his coronary blood flow was inadequate. When we called Rodney the next morning, he wanted to take Moshe back to the hospital by ambulance at once, but it was the Sabbath, and Moshe was now feeling much better, so he asked to stay at home until nightfall. Rodney agreed on condition that we call him immediately if the pain recurred. It did not, and Moshe returned to the hospital on Saturday evening.

An angiogram had been performed at the Shaare Zedek Medical Center on June 11, a week after Moshe was first hospitalized. It showed that all three of his coronary arteries were critically narrowed. The right coronary artery was in the worst shape. The only way to prevent a massive heart attack and to relieve Moshe's angina pectoris seemed to be triple bypass surgery.* Moshe's heart would not be beating during the bypass procedure; a heart-lung machine would perform his vital functions for him.

We were in the habit of weighing all our options carefully, but now there was little time in which to make a decision, and in fact there were no options. My brother Gershon, a physician in Los Angeles, had persuaded a friend, whom he described as "the best cardiac surgeon in L.A.," to postpone his vacation and carry out the operation the day after Moshe's arrival in that city. But Moshe was in no state to be flown anywhere, least of all on a twenty-two-hour trip. Not only would such a trip subject him to the stress of airport crowds and the possibility of delayed flights but, more important, planes are pressur-

*The surgeon would take a length of vein from his leg (veins are used because the diameter of a vein is larger than that of an artery) and graft it onto the coronary arteries above and below the obstructions, thereby making detours around them. This meant that Moshe's chest would be cut open and his chest bone sawn in two, in order to expose his heart.

ized to eight thousand feet, which somewhat reduces the supply of oxygen to the heart, and this might precipitate an attack of angina or even a heart attack.

There is only one cardiac surgery unit in Jerusalem; it is at Hadassah Hospital. Soon after Dr. Zangwill, chief of cardiology at Shaare Zedek, returned from abroad on June 17, he asked Dr. Benson, chief of cardiac surgery at Hadassah, to operate on Moshe as soon as possible. Surgery was scheduled for Monday, June 24. Dr. Zangwill assured us that Moshe was the ideal patient for a bypass operation because he had never had a heart attack, and the heart itself appeared to function normally. In any case, a coronary bypass is routine surgery nowadays. All of us—Moshe and I and our two sons, Alon and Jonathan —were optimistic, although we were aware that a small percentage of patients who undergo such surgery—about 3–5 percent a year in Israel—do not survive it. We knew that an angiogram is almost equally dangerous, however, and Moshe had tolerated that procedure well. We were not given *informed* consent specifying the many serious complications that can arise after coronary bypass surgery.

The husband of my good friend Krystyna, who had had a bypass in Milwaukee a few years earlier, was one of those unfortunate patients; he had died of complications a few weeks after the surgery. But Krystyna was the only person I knew well who could tell us what to expect. Knowing that doctors in the United States, unlike those in Israel, typically take great care to prepare all those involved for each step during and after the operation, I asked Krystyna to go through the details with us. I remember that we all joked a lot—one way to dispel anxiety.

Moshe had managed to retain his good spirits during the eighteen days of hospitalization before the surgery. He felt relieved to be monitored constantly. A professor of biblical philology and Semitic languages at Hebrew University, he had taken unfinished work with him; now at last he would be able to prepare his lecture for the International Congress of Judaic Studies, which he had helped to organize. At his bedside he had a novel by the Swiss writer Max Frisch, as well as some books in his field of study. He had little time for reading or writing; there was a constant stream of visitors, friends, and colleagues. He did, however, find time to draft his last will and testament. (Moshe had been to law school for two years and knew how to write the document.) Taking his responsibilities as head of the family seriously, he planned for the worst that might befall him.

Moshe was taken by ambulance to Hadassah Hospital on Sunday. Dr. Davies, the chief of anesthesiology, took Moshe's medical history and was so impressed by all the details Moshe knew about his illness and medication that he jokingly suggested that Moshe retrain and become a professor of cardiology. The boys and I spent that Sunday with him, and in the evening, Tamara, Alon's wife, smuggled their three-month-old baby into Moshe's room. We had a happy family party, but at the end of it Moshe said: "Tomorrow everything is going to go wrong." Of course I tried to talk him out of his gloomy mood, never imagining for a moment that he might be having a premonition of things to come. Dr. Davies had advised me not to see Moshe the next morning prior to the surgery, so as to avoid a stressful farewell scene. Moshe agreed. In fact Moshe suggested that I see my own patients as usual and that I come to the hospital only near the anticipated end of the operation.

My friend Naama, a nurse, visited Moshe later that evening and reported admiringly that she had never before seen a patient who spent the hours before undergoing major surgery correcting proofs for a scholarly article. Moshe did not like to waste time! On the operating table the next morning he reportedly said: "I am not frightened—I am going over to the other side."

During one of my sessions with a patient on Monday morning, the phone rang. Our friend David, an immunologist, had phoned the operating room and had been informed that everything was going smoothly. I was calm and confident.

At midday I entered the waiting room with the boys and my uncle Werner. Surely, when Sartre wrote No Exit, his play about hell, he must have had such a room in mind. It had two doors but no windows. One door was always open, allowing relatives and friends of patients to come and go. When many operations are taking place, people overflow into the corridor, which has the advantage of a window. The other door of the waiting room was kept closed. The guard opened it for only two reasons: to admit the white-coated woman volunteer whose task it was to read out the names of patients who had awakened after their surgery, and to allow relatives into the corridor leading to the recovery rooms.

You can imagine the tense atmosphere of the waiting room, punctuated by moments of alert expectation when the woman volunteer made her appearance. During the morning hours the waiting room is usually filled to capacity. Gradually, as patients awake from their surgery, it empties.

An hour after my arrival the anesthesiologist looked in at the second door to tell us that Moshe's bypass had just been completed and that the surgeons would need about an hour and a half to close the chest. We were all relieved. Uncle Werner went home to phone the good news to my mother in London.

Naama had warned me that the closing of the chest would probably take longer than ninety minutes, so I was not particularly disturbed that Moshe was still in the operating room three hours later. I even joked feebly to my sons that Moshe's obesity was to blame for the fact that closing the chest was taking longer than anticipated. Another hour passed. It was five o'clock when Dr. Davies finally called me. It appeared that the doctors had encountered difficulties getting Moshe's heart to beat again after he had been taken off the heart-lung machine. Dr. Davies promised to report again in about an hour.

I was stunned. This was the first time I was forced to confront the possibility that things could end badly.

I ran to the nearest pay phone and called Rodney. Twenty minutes later he was in the waiting room with us, even though it meant leaving his wife, ill with flu, alone with their baby.

I also called David, the immunologist, on the house phone, and he too came to the waiting room at once. He paced up and down the corridor, looking very serious, smoking his pipe. As the hours passed without further news I suggested that he phone into the operating room again. He was adamant in his refusal, insisting that the doctors would need all their concentration to save Moshe's life. Communicating with us would only divert their attention from the vital task.

My cousin Itamar joined us, and later Tamara, Alon's wife; Judy, David's wife; and Yona, Jonathan's girlfriend. The boys were quietly reciting psalms. I wept for the first time as I visualized the possibility that Moshe could die. My world seemed to be collapsing. I tried unsuccessfully not to think about it, to dismiss it from my mind. But my terror mounted. My mouth was dry and my stomach seemed tied in knots. I wanted to scream but how could I, surrounded by my family and friends, enclosed in that windowless hell? I could not allow my panic to infect the others. I had to find some way to calm myself. In the past, music had served as a kind of tranquilizer for me, so I turned on my radio headset and listened to a Bruckner symphony.

My life with Moshe passed before my mind's eye. Our first meeting was thirty-three years earlier in London, where I had heard him lecture about the three monotheistic religions. He had just arrived from Jerusalem and was on his way to Oxford for a year's sabbatical. A short while thereafter we met at a workshop he taught on Hebrew language and literature. We soon fell in love and after a few months decided to get married. As a lecturer at the Hebrew University, Moshe had to return to Israel for the following academic year. I was in a quandary since I had just been accepted for a year's internship in abnormal psychology at the Institute of Psychiatry, Maudsley Hospital, London. Moshe was convinced that I should complete my professional training before coming to Israel and persuaded me to remain in London after our wedding.

At last we settled down in Jerusalem, and after a few years our two sons were born.

Moshe primarily taught ancient Semitic languages like Syriac, Aramaic, and Ugaritic. He also edited a large dictionary of modern Hebrew. Later he added new projects, such as the scientific edition of the book of Isaiah and a modern Arab–Hebrew dictionary. His numerous articles, books, and scientific projects had gained him an international reputation; he was at the top of his career.

Meanwhile, I had earned my doctorate, after which I devoted my energies to the department of child psychiatry at Hadassah, where I treated children and their parents. Later I directed a research project dealing with multiple births and joined the faculty of Bar Ilan University.

Thus we were both busy people, involved in our personal and professional lives, but never neglecting the social and cultural aspects of Jerusalem.

In 1958, Moshe was invited to act as a consultant on Jewish matters for Metro Goldwyn Mayer during the filming of *Ben Hur* in Rome. So Moshe, Alon, and I lived in Rome for four glorious months. Two years later, just after Jonathan's birth, we went to Boston for Moshe's sabbatical. Moshe taught at Brandeis University, and I worked at the Judge Baker Guidance Center. There followed numerous vacations and sabbaticals in many different countries. But most of our life was spent in Jerusalem. The boys grew into young men, and Alon started a family of his own. We felt that life was good to us. Was all this about to come to an abrupt end in the nearby operating room?

These were the recollections and thoughts that raced through my head while I sat in the waiting room.

By early evening, only our family and friends were left in the waiting room; there were no relatives or friends of other patients. This fact added to my concern that some unforeseen complication was occurring.

At 8:00 P.M. Dr. Davies, the anesthesiologist, appeared and said that the situation had improved: Moshe's heart was beating more vigorously. Another hour passed before we were told that the operation was completed. My relief knew no bounds.

Soon after, Dr. Benson, the surgeon, gave us a detailed report. I was too excited to understand it and later asked Rodney to repeat the story in plain English:

Twice after the completion of the bypass, Moshe had to be returned to the heart-lung machine because his heart did not beat strongly enough and his blood pressure had dropped profoundly. This was associated with a mitral valve leak which caused the blood to flow back into the cardiac chamber instead of to the major arteries. The surgeon had to wait until what turned out to be a functional disturbance corrected itself.

The cause of these events was not clear at the time, but in retrospect they appear to have been related to a heart attack which had occurred during the operation but had gone unrecognized.* Only

---

*Dr. Elkhonon Goldberg, a neurologist who examined Moshe in New York in January 1988, believes that Moshe also suffered from a minor stroke during that operation, which had likewise gone undetected.

after the surgeon had inserted a temporary balloon pump to aid the heart's functioning was it possible to stabilize Moshe's blood pressure. Although Moshe's survival had been touch and go for a while, the final outcome was promising: now his heart was beating more vigorously, and the mitral valve that had leaked had become functional; two of the three grafts were successful. At present Moshe was still unconscious, but I was allowed to look at him in the recovery room.

Dressed in a white gown with a surgical mask and dust covers for my shoes, I entered the recovery room but could hardly see Moshe among the forest of tubes and machines. There was not only the respirator to help him breathe and the balloon pump that helped his heart to beat and improved the flow of blood to the vital organs, but also innumerable tubes coming out of his body and diverse fluids dripping into his veins. Above his head various monitors reflected his vital signs, displaying an array of ever-changing numbers. It was an awesome sight and not one that enabled me to relate in a personal way to the patient on the bed, who was my husband. Trying to restrain my tears, I left after ten minutes. When Dr. Benson invited me to go back for another visit a little later, I declined: I preferred to wait until Moshe had recovered consciousness.

Alon went in to see his father soon after I left and stayed there for a while. He seemed to take it in his stride; later, outside the recovery room, he was making plans with Dr. Benson to take him on a synagogue tour of the Old City once Moshe had recovered. I discouraged Jonathan, who is extremely sensitive, from seeing Moshe in his present condition and suggested he wait until Moshe had awakened.

I left my phone number with the doctor on duty in the recovery room so that he could call me as soon as Moshe woke up. I then went home to catch a few hours' sleep, hopeful that everything would be as it should the next morning. I called the recovery room every two hours during the night.

In bed that night, I recalled that my brother Gershon had phoned from Los Angeles three days before Moshe's operation, imploring us to use a particular cardiac surgeon whose praises he had sung. Even though I knew that his intentions were the best, I felt that Gershon was putting me in an impossible situation at a time when all our decisions had already been made. When I needed reassurance, he infused me not only with doubt but also with feelings of guilt. I argued with him over the phone for a long time but remained adamant in my refusal to make any changes in the arrangements for Moshe's bypass, since our choice of surgeons had the backing of medical friends whose opinions I respected.

Now I allowed my imagination to roam freely. What if? Would the scenario have been different if the roles had been played by different actors? After a while I comforted myself with the belief that it was due to the skill of the surgeons in the Hadassah operating room that Moshe's life had been saved the previous day.

Moshe had still not awakened by morning. The doctor suggested that I come in and call Moshe by his name—perhaps my familiar voice would have the desired effect. But my efforts at arousing him were futile. I was told that with the strong anesthetics needed for a twelve-hour operation, it might take up to forty-eight hours for Moshe to come round. Alon and I went in to see him periodically during this and the following day. We saw him make a few spontaneous movements: he moved all his limbs except his left leg, which he could not move even in response to doctors' requests to do so. We were assured these were significant signs that he was no longer so deeply unconscious.

❖

From the time it became apparent that Moshe's operation was far from uneventful, I felt surrounded by love. Neither Alon nor Jonathan would leave my side. They expressed their concern and sympathy not only physically, by holding my hand, but also through their glances and words. I can no longer recapture those words exactly, but their gist is unforgettable: "Your pain and worry are ours. We are all in this together, and with God's help we shall overcome." They instilled in me their deep confidence and hope for a positive outcome. Through their strength I grew strong. I was proud to have such sons, especially in those dark hours.

Yona, Jonathan's girlfriend, behaved like a member of the family, bringing me food for my return from the hospital. Although I could not swallow anything solid then or during the days that followed, I was grateful to her for trying to take care of my unexpressed physical needs.

We were fortunate that Rodney lived in our building at this time of medical crisis. "Call me any time, even if you wake up at 3 A.M. and want to talk to somebody. I'll come down to you. After all, I am a doctor and am used to being called at night," he generously offered. He was available to talk to me daily about events at the hospital and to answer my questions. He also welcomed phone calls from my friends and relatives abroad who wanted to get a report straight from a doctor's mouth even though he was not the doctor in charge. I felt that he represented a vanishing breed of physicians who have their hearts in the right place—not a bad quality in a cardiologist.

# 2

# Coma

Forty-eight hours passed. Moshe had not yet awakened. On Thursday, the third day after surgery, the cardiac surgeon told me that Moshe would need another operation to remove a large blood clot (hematoma) that had formed in his chest. More morphium would have to be administered as an anesthetic, countering our efforts to awaken Moshe. Another vigil with relatives and friends followed. The second operation lasted for four hours. Afterward Moshe's coma deepened, and he did not react to such painful stimuli as the surgeon's hitting his chest or pricking him with a needle. Nor did he move any part of his body spontaneously.* His state fit the description of coma given by Fred Plum and Jerome B. Posner in *The Diagnosis of Stupor and Coma* (1981, p. 355): "a continuous, unarousable, eyes-closed unconscious-

---

*The type of damage Moshe was thought to have sustained is often associated with spontaneous movements in the first few days after the operation, followed by deterioration on the third day, so that the apparent increase and then deterioration in consciousness would probably have occurred even without the second surgical intervention.

ness with the patient giving no response to verbal stimulation and no localizing or appropriately resisting motor responses." He scored 3 on the Glasgow coma scale, signifying that he was in the deepest coma possible.

The anesthesiologist explained to us that the blood supply to Moshe's brain during the first operation had been inadequate. Decreased oxygen delivery to the brain (anoxia) had damaged the brain and caused the coma. The reduced blood flow was probably related to the fact that after the grafts had been completed and attempts were made to restore Moshe's myocardial function, his heart beat too weakly to send sufficient blood to the vital organs. Moshe's blood pressure remained dangerously low during this period. The duration of the coma would depend on the amount of brain damage he had suffered as a result of the anoxia. If the brain cells had died, the situation was irreversible. If they had merely been injured they might sooner or later recover and function again.*

Dr. Davies pointed out one encouraging sign: Moshe was breathing spontaneously. Alon comforted himself with the thought that if Moshe awoke a few days hence, he would at least have been spared the acute pain that follows bypass surgery. Dr. Davies agreed that this might be the one positive feature associated with the coma—a novel way of seeing it, he thought. But a week after the operation, Moshe was still in the deepest possible coma. A CAT scan of the brain performed six days after the first operation ruled out a blood clot or swelling due to accumulation of fluids. The scan was normal. We were told, however, that a CAT scan may not show any abnormality in the first two weeks following anoxic brain damage. Moreover, it was possible that Moshe's unconsciousness was caused by a lesion too small to be revealed by a CAT scan.

There was nothing the doctors could do to hasten Moshe's awakening. Nor did Dr. Davies think that auditory stimulation via talk

*The late Canadian neurosurgeon Wilder Penfield showed that no one area in the cortex can be singled out as essential for consciousness. Even extensive damage to the cortex will not impair consciousness. But the cortex must be aroused by signals from a part of the brainstem called the reticular activating system (RAS). A permanently damaged RAS means irreversible coma.

or radio would help accelerate Moshe's recovery. He advised us to resume some of our usual activities and not to spend all day long at the patient's side.

In the evening of day thirteen after the first operation, Alon received me at the hospital with wonderful news: Moshe had opened his right eye! I rushed in to witness this event for myself. A few days later Moshe opened his left eye as well, but he clearly was not seeing or focusing with either eye; he was still in a deep coma. The eyes moved in an uncoordinated fashion; sometimes one eye was open, sometimes the other. However, there was a rhythm of eye opening and closing corresponding to a rhythm of wakefulness and sleep. Moshe did not respond to painful stimulation of his upper limbs but there was some response to pain in the lower limbs. The doctors considered him to be "in a vegetative state."* But we were reassured to know that Moshe was not brain dead since he could breathe and open and close his eyes.

The worst part of this situation for me was the fact that the doctors were utterly helpless to do anything to awaken Moshe. We are all reared to believe in the efficacy of the medical profession, so the realization that the doctors could contribute absolutely nothing to Moshe's recovery came as a total shock.

Having almost magical expectations that the top physicians might be able to help Moshe, I called them in to see him. The head neurologist, Dr. Finkel, and the chief of internal medicine, Dr. Schwarz, looked down at the floor when they saw me. They had nothing to say. When these scientists did speak, it was of the need for God's mercy! This could mean only one thing: in their opinion the situation was hopeless, and there was nothing they could do to relieve it.

Shlomi, a resident in neurosurgery, at whose wedding Moshe had appeared while on leave from the intensive coronary unit, examined Moshe and read his case notes. He grimly advised us not to hover at

*Vegetative state is a medical term referring to a condition in which both cerebral hemispheres (the parts of the brain dealing with cognition) are severely damaged whereas the brain stem, which controls breathing and some reflexes, is functioning. When prolonged anoxia leads to unconsciousness in which only the vegetative state is achieved after sixteen days, this usually indicates that many areas of the brain have been affected.

Moshe's bedside. He even suggested moving Moshe to Bet Levenstein, a hospital near Tel Aviv for neurologically damaged patients. We refused to accept this advice, feeling that Moshe was receiving the best possible care in his present environment.

Despite the apparent hopelessness of the situation, Moshe's cardiac surgeon exhorted us not to give up hope. He told us of patients who had awakened after prolonged coma and regained their abilities; one of these was an eighty-year-old woman. Dr. Davies, the anesthesiologist, also cited cases in the medical literature of patients who had recovered after a long coma. I became a magnet for stories of such miraculous recoveries all over the world and an eager listener to each of them. Moshe's cousin Ursel called from Berlin to tell me that her maid's mother had awakened after a three-month coma; the wife of another heart surgery patient, whose husband had been unconscious for five weeks, encouraged us not to lose hope; my mother's physician in London reported his positive experiences with formerly comatose patients. The bottom line of all these stories, which helped to keep our hopes alive, was that Moshe's full recovery was possible.

Another way to dispel our despair at the neurologist's dire predictions was to doubt his ability to understand the brain. We were strengthened in this seemingly irrational attitude by Natan, an Israeli virologist of world renown, who implored me not to give credence to the neurological forecasts of doom. Natan had had a stroke seven months previously and had lost the power of speech together with the ability to move his right leg. His neurologists had doubted that he would ever be able to talk again, and here he was speaking in three languages! Nor did they think he would regain the use of his right leg sufficiently to walk, as he did now without any difficulty.

It was comforting to hear Natan's story, and he easily converted me to his optimistic frame of mind; in fact, I decided to avoid all neurologists since it was they who had given Moshe the worst prognosis.

❖

I was overcome by a strange sense of déjà vu. A dozen years earlier, my father, then aged seventy-four years, was at the terminal stage of his long illness. He had suffered a number of small strokes over more than twenty years, and he had finally been reduced to a vegetative state. He had become totally dependent on others for all his basic needs and he also reacted less and less frequently to people around him. My mother had refused to move him to a hospital, choosing instead to look after him at home with the help of visiting nurses. Although she had the support of my sister, her husband, my brother in London—and occasionally mine—the main burden had been hers, and she had borne it with admirable fortitude. I felt as if I were being tested as she had been. But my father had suffered from an irreversible process. My hope was that since Moshe's condition was the result of an acute trauma, it could be reversed.

The father of a young girl who had just had heart surgery stood next to me in the recovery room. He looked extremely anxious. "Has she woken up already?" I inquired. She had. I told him how fortunate she was, adding that my husband was still unconscious after three weeks. He looked at me full of sympathy. "Have you checked the texts of your *mezuzot*? Maybe they are imperfect." (Mezuzot are parchment scrolls containing biblical texts, fixed to every doorpost in Jewish households.) I resented his simplistic faith, which implied a connection between Moshe's coma and our failure to observe a religious precept flawlessly. I turned away.

Nevertheless, while there seemed reason to despair, there were sparks of hope to which we clung tenaciously. Alon, Jonathan, and I continued to visit Moshe daily, each of us at a different time of the day. We told him about current events in our lives, since we had heard of comatose patients waking up and remembering what had happened during the coma. Because it was conceivable that he was able to hear us but not to communicate, we made sure not to mention anything negative about his condition or its prognosis in his presence. I would go in for fifteen minutes, then take a break to rest and cry about my sheer helplessness, returning several times for more of the same. Alon made a habit of praying at Moshe's bedside.

Family and close friends were always ready to cheer me up in the time out I took from visiting Moshe or to accompany me patiently during those hours and days of vigils. My daughter-in-law, Tamara, brought baby Elisha to the Hadassah garden by the pool almost every morning. (We were not allowed to use the hospital lounge, which was reserved for overseas guests of the Hadassah organization.) Whenever I took a break from Moshe's bedside I would find new faces beside Tamara's. Everyone who knew me and had heard about Moshe's operation spent some time at my side, comforting me. Some drove me home for lunch, others transported me to the hospital in the morning, and still others, like Adena, sat with us throughout Moshe's second operation. They made me feel as if they also suffered my pain and wanted to ease it in whatever way possible.

Though Moshe's neurological problems were critical, there was no shortage of other medical complications. He stopped passing urine and developed respiratory and urinary tract infections and cardiac arrhythmia; one of his wounds ulcerated, and he had two large bed-sores. He required twenty-three pints of blood (donated by relatives and friends of the family) to replace blood lost through his wounds after his first operation. His sheets were blood-drenched during those first days. It seemed that anything that could go wrong did. His condition became critical on several occasions. This was vividly brought home to me seven days after his second operation, when the doctors again asked for my home phone number as I was leaving: as a result of Moshe's severe urinary infection, which was likely to cause kidney failure, the doctors expected the worst. But once again his life was saved.

Only many weeks later did I realize with horror that at the time Israel had no provisions for testing blood for the AIDS virus. Had Moshe's life been spared only for him to succumb to this modern plague? Overcome by anxiety, I called Dr. Benson. "There are only a few AIDS patients in Israel, so you can relax on that account," he reassured me. Yet I could not entirely shake off my worry; much later, I persuaded a doctor to test Moshe's blood for AIDS and obtained the desired negative result.

A week after his severe urinary infection, Moshe seemed to have great difficulties breathing. He sounded as if he were throttling, and I feared his end was near. I called Osnat, the nurse who was primarily in charge of Moshe. After observing him for a short while, she asked me to leave the recovery room (which served as an intensive coronary unit for chest surgery patients). When I reappeared a half hour later (I was usually allowed in at all times unless there was an emergency or a new case being admitted from the operating room) she sent me out again, adding that I should not return until told to do so.

I sat in the waiting room for an hour, then for another hour, my anxiety growing by leaps and bounds. I tried to obtain information from the nurses' aide, but she had no message for me. At last Naama passed the waiting room on her way home. I shared my fears with her, and she immediately changed back into her nursing uniform in order to find out what was going on. Returning from the recovery room ten minutes later, she told me that the admission of two new post-surgical patients had kept the nurses busy and that I could now come in to see Moshe. I was reassured when I saw him breathing peacefully, but I felt very angry that I had been left to stew in anxiety. Two days later I gathered sufficient composure to tell Osnat what my expulsion from the recovery room, and her failure to communicate with me, had done to my nerves. Osnat maintained that Moshe had indeed had serious breathing problems which she had needed to take care of. Even so, I suggested to her that in the event of any future emergency, she should at least communicate in some way with the visiting relatives, who, I felt, were entitled to this basic right.

❖ ❖ ❖ 3 ❖ ❖ ❖

# Miracle Drug

The phone rang at midnight. It was my mother calling from London. She had talked with Dr. Aron, her physician, about Moshe, and he had apparently expressed shock that nothing was being done to get Moshe out of his ten-day-long coma. He had seen good results in comatose patients with a combination of Nootropil, a Belgian drug, and Parentrovite, a high-potency compound of vitamins B and C. The combination was said to stimulate the nerve cells and to increase the blood supply to the brain. Dr. Aron assured my mother that should this drug turn out to be ineffective, it would at least do no harm.

I was heartened by the possibility of doing something for Moshe. At 6:45 the next morning I called Dr. Benson, the cardiac surgeon, to ask if he would give his consent to have the drug administered to Moshe. (He never complained about my calls to him at home and, in fact, with unfailing courtesy, never neglected to thank me for having phoned.) He agreed to consult his neurological colleagues and later that day gave me the green light to obtain the drug, which was unavailable in Israel.

My brother-in-law David, who lives in London, made inquiries at his local synagogue and located a woman who was flying to Israel that evening. She was willing to bring the medicine to me in Jerusalem. Meanwhile, Dr. Aron wrote an accompanying letter to the security personnel at Heathrow and Lydda airports describing the contents of the package so that they would not think it contained explosives.

Thirty hours after the first phone call from my mother, the drug was in my hands. I raced with it to the chief of neurology, Dr. Finkel, but was crestfallen when he said that he had never injected Nootropil; he had only used it in tablet form for Alzheimer's disease. Since Dr. Aron had not enclosed instructions on how to inject the drug, Dr. Finkel did not know how to proceed.

Innumerable phone calls to and from London followed: via my mother we contacted Dr. Aron, who then tried unsuccessfully to reach Dr. Finkel throughout the day. Finally we asked Dr. Aron to call Dr. Benson, the cardiac surgeon, and give him the exact instructions. This done, the new course of therapy started. For the following month Moshe received regular daily injections of the drug and vitamins.

Since the original supply of Nootropil was insufficient, I obtained further ampules through my friend Latzi, who had flown to Belgium on business. He persuaded a pharmacist there to sell him the Nootropil although he had no prescription for it. I also insisted on having a further consignment of Parentrovite flown in from England, since I wanted to make sure that the vitamins Moshe was getting were composed in exactly the same way that Dr. Aron had originally specified. The local Israeli brand of vitamins did not satisfy me. Again David found a tourist willing to transport these capsules. My friends Shirley and Bill met the flight that evening and collected the parcel for me. For my own peace of mind it was crucial that I leave no stone unturned in trying to help Moshe.

The family attributed any slight improvement in Moshe's state to this "miracle drug." The doctors, however, were skeptical. They did not think the Nootropil had any beneficial effect. Dr. Benson even feared that repeated injections of the drug might be responsible for the fever Moshe had had for several days.

At this time, there had been no controlled studies of the effectiveness of Nootropil for the treatment of coma. The doctors in Jerusalem were relying on the unsubstantiated claims of a physician whom they did not even know. Later, one of them commented that if a drug with proven beneficial effects on coma had really existed, it would have been known worldwide in the medical community.

Our use of Nootropil can be compared to the use of Laetril by patients with cancer. Laetril had an unproven reputation for effectiveness in some cancer patients. However, when it was subjected to clinical trials, no evidence of its efficacy was found. No such clinical trials have ever been attempted for Nootropil, but we were anxious to clutch at any straw. The greater the difficulty in obtaining the drug, the better we felt. The greater our exertion, the greater our need to believe that Moshe was responding.

## Hope and Despair

In times of peak emotion, whether of ecstasy or misery, I always turn to the great writers and poets to find an expression for my incoherent feelings. I was not disappointed. Homer had put into the mouths of his protagonists the awesome question I faced: to believe or not to believe in the return of the hero. Would Odysseus come back to his family? The two opposing voices that fought ceaselessly within my mind were externalized in the *Odyssey*. Telemachus, son of Odysseus and the goddess Athena, seemed to express my despair in the following lines:

"But he is lost: he came to grief and perished
and there's no help for us in someone's hoping he
still may come . . ."

The goddess replied in words of comfort, reflecting my own hopes:

"I see the gods delay him. But never in this world
is Odysseus dead—only detained somewhere in the
white sea, upon some island, with wild islanders . . ."

Telemachus also mirrored my cautious optimism most aptly:

"If he's alive and beating his way home I might
hold out for another weary year . . ."

To hope or not to hope, that was the question. It was easier to despair,
to give up, to join the ranks of almost all the doctors who had seen
Moshe. One of Moshe's former consultants, who had been abroad for
a sabbatical, represented the majority opinion when he said to me,
after visiting Moshe in the ward and reading his chart: "I understand
there is hope but no chance" for his recovery.

I protested that this was not how I perceived the situation. Later,
when I recalled the scene, I wondered who had given him the right to
express his unasked-for opinion, which gnawed at my tenuous hopes.
Did he feel it necessary to describe the facts so brutally in order to
make me face "reality"? Yet he was one of the few physicians who
visited Moshe at home once he had recovered consciousness. Both
then and on later occasions he asked me whether I remembered what
he had said at Moshe's bedside when he was in a coma.

How could I separate myself physically and emotionally from
Moshe and relate to him as a has-been when he was still alive and
breathing? After all, there *were* people who had recovered from deep
coma after a stroke, or gunshot wound to the head, or brain injury sustained in a car accident. Some of these people functioned
reasonably well thereafter.

It was comforting to be lulled by nonmedical friends who argued:
"Moshe has such an unusual brain that even if certain cells have been
irreversibly damaged, there are enough remaining cells that can take
over." But could the function of dead cells be replaced by living ones?

Time was of the essence, we were repeatedly told. The pessimists thought no sign of intelligence could survive a deep coma of ten days' duration. The optimists insisted that the patient might recuperate as long as he or she awoke from the coma within twelve months. But most believed that the longer the coma, the greater the permanent impairment of functions. With these diverse opinions it became clear that I would have to walk a tightrope between hope and despair throughout the duration of Moshe's coma.

Dreams can be such great restorers! Isca, a psychotherapist friend in London, asked me four weeks after Moshe's surgery whether I had been able to dream at all. I realized that I did not remember having dreamed throughout this traumatic period. Probably my sleep was too fitful for that.

But two nights after I received Isca's letter, I had the following dream: "I am depressed and Shirley comforts me." I felt relieved when I woke up.

Shirley, a poet, is a very warm friend, full of sympathy. Even in my dire situation, she was able to console me in my dream. Surely there can be no consolation without hope, I thought. With the help of this dream some of my hope was restored to me.

# ❖ ❖ ❖ 5 ❖ ❖ ❖
## Faith

"Out of the depths have I cried unto thee, oh Lord." The words of the psalmist turning to God for help are still relevant in any seemingly hopeless situation. Even the physicians had spoken of the need for God's intervention in order to restore Moshe to us.

Alon, throughout these difficult weeks, implored me to believe in the Almighty, who could be trusted to return Moshe to us in good health. If only one could will one's faith!

I was determined not to bargain with God; there was going to be no "If Thou wilt give Moshe back to me safe and sound I will . . ." Such a bargain reminded me of Jeptha, who promised to sacrifice the first living creature he encountered on his way home if God enabled him to win a battle. The creature turned out to be his own daughter, who welcomed him on his return! Such bargains are too risky; one can never tell in advance where they will lead.

Traditional Jews recite psalms whenever anyone's life is in danger. Many of Moshe's friends and relatives all over the world read psalms daily on his behalf once the news was out that he had not awakened from his operation.

There is also a special blessing, a *Mee She'berach,* uttered in synagogue on behalf of a critically ill person. The patient is identified by name as the son of his mother rather than the son of his father. (This is because, theoretically, paternity is always doubtful.) I received dozens of phone calls from friends requesting the name of Moshe's mother. All of them wanted to make a Mee She'berach for Moshe ben Devora.

I frequently heard the comment: "Moshe *must* recover—so many people are praying for him." It was as if the more people implored God on his behalf, the more likely God was to answer their prayers.

When matters get really desperate, observant Jews sometimes use a special method to counteract the death sentence that is presumed to have been passed on the ill person by God's Court of Law. This method involves changing the person's name. By receiving a new name, he or she becomes a new person, one who has not been sentenced to die. Changing the patient's name also changes the divine decree from illness to health. A name such as Chaim ("life") or Rephael ("let God cure") or Hezekiah (a king of Judah who recovered from a serious illness) is usually chosen.

About two weeks after Moshe's surgery, Jonathan called upon roughly thirty relatives, friends, and colleagues to meet at the Western Wall—for Jews the holiest place in the world since the destruction of the Temple. They recited psalms in unison; then Jonathan announced that Moshe's name had been changed to Hezekiah—Chizkiyahu in Hebrew. Many people sighed in relief once the renaming ceremony had taken place. For them it was as if Moshe had been born again as Chizkiyahu.

❖

In times of uncertainty one clutches at straws. Where science throws up its hands in ignorance and impotence, the mystical takes over. It was reported to me that an employee of the Hebrew University had consulted a kabbalist (mystic) about Moshe's condition. The kabbalist was said to be able to discover the future through studying certain texts. He predicted that if Moshe survived week two, with all its medical emergencies, he would recover. I eagerly lapped up this prophecy.

# Change of Scene

Moshe survived many life-endangering complications and, though still in a coma, he was moved into a five-bed room of the cardiac surgery ward four weeks after his bypass operation.

Normally patients are transferred from the recovery room to the cardiac surgery ward about three days after surgery. One of the Hadassah physicians told me he had never heard of a patient remaining in the recovery room as long as four weeks. There were days when Moshe was the only patient there, yet his surgeon allowed him to remain in this expensive facility with two nurses on duty around the clock and a doctor always present or on call. For this I shall always be grateful to him.

Three weeks after the operation Dr. Benson asked us to acquire an air mattress for Moshe to use in the cardiac surgery ward, to help prevent the formation of bedsores. Moshe already had two bedsores although he was supposed to be regularly turned and massaged on the air mattress in the recovery room.

Yad Sarah is a medical equipment loan society. I called to see if they had such a mattress, but they were out of stock. I secretly hoped that if I did not procure the mattress, Moshe would stay in the recovery room until he awoke from his coma. Yet deep down I knew that this was a false hope. I managed to locate an air mattress in the Haifa branch of Yad Sarah. Moshe's colleague and former student, Yeshaya, who lives in Haifa, procured the mattress and sent it to Jerusalem in a taxi.

The idea of Moshe's being returned to a ward, no longer under constant medical and nursing surveillance while in a comatose state, frightened me. It meant that the boys and I would have to spend more time at the hospital and try to get friends to help out at other hours of the day. This was a task too great for our small family if we wanted to continue with some semblance of normal life. But eager friends, students, and colleagues generously offered their time and energy, and I welcomed them all.

Yet inviting all these people into Moshe's ward meant allowing them to encroach on the family's privacy. They would see us at our most vulnerable. On one occasion Yaacov, a colleague of Moshe's, was present when a nurse spoke harshly to me. It was the last straw—I burst into tears. Since I did not know Yaacov very well, I walked out into the corridor to spare him the sight of my tears. When I returned to Moshe's bedside, Yaacov had gone. Later he told Alon that he had thought I might not feel comfortable with him in such a situation. Unfortunately, not everyone was as tactful as he.

One piece of medical equipment was conspicuously absent in this ward: the bedrail that prevents the patient from falling out of bed. I was afraid that Moshe might fall, land on the floor, and fracture his hip, necessitating further surgery and anesthesia. When I mentioned this to the nurses they assured me that Moshe was immobile and did not require a bedrail. I remained unconvinced. I begged them to pro-cure a bedrail for my peace of mind if not for Moshe's physical safety. They made only half-hearted attempts to obtain one. When I realized that I was not getting very far in my endeavors, I decided to put my request before Dr. Benson. Like the nurses, he could not envisage Moshe, in his comatose condition, falling out of bed, but I begged him to go along with what seemed to them to be my irrational fears. The following day the bedrail had been installed. Twenty-four hours later I saw both of his legs dangling through the rail, out of his bed. I sighed with relief: surely my obstinacy had spared us all unnecessary complications.

In the cardiac surgery ward, Moshe was no longer constantly monitored, and he was also taken off the basic life support system (the respirator and balloon pump). Apart from a small oxygen mask, the intravenous fluids, the nasogastric tube, and a urinary catheter, Moshe's body functioned unaided. Five weeks after his surgery he was propped up in a chair for several hours daily to help his lungs drain. At first, like a newborn infant, he could not support his head in an upright position; it flopped from side to side or fell forward onto his chin. But two or three weeks later he was able to right his head and gradually to sit upright. By the time he left that ward after ten weeks, he looked ready to get out of the chair.

Moshe needed far more nursing care and attention than the other patients in the ward because he was totally helpless. He could do absolutely nothing for himself, not even turn in bed. The nurses were wonderful, but they were terribly overworked since there were always too few of them and Moshe's needs were too many.

I have a poor memory for names, but I struggled to learn the name of each nurse who was looking after Moshe. I believed that these efforts might help the nurses feel that I related to them on a personal basis and that they in turn would relate to Moshe and my family as individuals. It turned out to be energy well invested. One nurse who will always remain in my memory was Chana. She had recently emigrated to Israel from Chicago, though her accent when she spoke English—she knew very little Hebrew—was that of a recent arrival from Eastern Europe. She had, in fact, been born in Israel, but her Yiddish-speaking parents, originally from Poland, had taken her to the United States as a child. I was intrigued by her life story, and she was always ready to put in extra time and effort with Moshe. She became "our" nurse, and we, likewise, became "her" family.

Because there was too much work and too few hands to carry it out, I was cautious in summoning a nurse to Moshe's bedside. I had to decide whether my request was urgent, especially if it came at the time of the nurses' coffee or lunch break, and whether I might annoy the nurses, which would be counterproductive. I also had to learn quickly which of the nurses resented making the extra effort required and which did not.

The family members helped care for Moshe in the ward. We called a nurse when the intravenous tube was obstructed and when the oxygen mask on Moshe's face needed repositioning. Moshe needed to be turned in bed every two hours, and this necessitated the help of two nurses. Sometimes he slid down in the chair in which he was propped up. Since each of us visited him alone at a different time of the day, we could not handle these situations without the nurses' help.

Frequently I was rebuked by one or another nurse with: "He is not our only patient." I was well aware of this but, on the other hand, I thought: he *is* my only husband, and his needs are greater than those of his fellow patients. After all, it was not his fault that he did not wake up after surgery, whereas all the other patients did.

It no doubt appeared to Moshe's fellow patients and their visitors that he received an inordinate amount of the nurses' time and attention. Yet none of them ever complained about it. On the contrary, they watched him with great sympathy. Some even monitored Moshe for signs of progress, which they eagerly reported to us. The families of these patients, who slept by their sides during the first days after surgery, also rejoiced when they saw any improvement in Moshe's condition. At times other patients' spouses or children even helped Moshe by moistening his lips or calling a nurse when he seemed to require aid.

Only one woman, protective of her husband, grumbled at the amount of nursing attention Moshe required. She complained that light and noise in his corner during the night prevented her husband from getting his sleep. To me she expressed her sympathy, but she added that her husband was also extremely ill and that someone as sick as Moshe should surely lie in a room by himself. I pointed out that there were no single rooms in Hadassah. When she suggested that the television room be turned into a private room for Moshe, I told her to forward her ideas to Dr. Benson. A few days later her husband was moved to a different ward.

On one occasion, when Moshe's face was covered with perspiration, the nurse took his temperature under the arm, where it registered normal. Later I saw him soaked in sweat, and his forehead was really hot. I asked the nurse to take his temperature again. She was reluctant, since Moshe had recently been seen by a doctor. But I prevailed on her to take his temperature, this time rectally. He turned out to have a high fever whose cause had to be investigated and treated at once. Fortunately, Moshe did not have pneumonia, an embolism, or any of the other dreaded possibilities. He "merely" had a urinary infection.

I was mercifully unaware of all the possible diagnoses that the doctors had to rule out. One evening Alon received me with glad tidings: "Dad does not have meningitis." Even the thought made me shudder. It turned out that, because of Moshe's prolonged fever and his comatose state, the neurologist had performed a spinal tap to test for this fearful ailment.

There were constantly new causes for concern. About eight weeks after Moshe's surgery, one of his former students, Miriam, phoned me to express her distress about Moshe's condition. She told me that her recently deceased mother had survived three brain operations in two years, only to succumb to bedsores. She implored me to have Moshe's bedsores taken care of. Moshe now had three of them, two on his buttocks and one at the back of his head. In spite of the conscientious ministrations of the nurses and the special mattress, none of these sores was healing properly.

I ran in consternation to Tsippy, the head nurse. I had never realized before that bedsores could be so serious.

"How old was your friend's mother? In her eighties?" Tsippy asked.

"Probably."

"And how old is your husband?" she continued. "At least twenty years younger?"

I agreed.

"Tell the woman not to worry you unnecessarily. The situation is quite different in a younger person," she concluded.

I was not satisfied. "When will Moshe finally be rid of these bedsores?" I insisted on knowing.

"Once he is able to get around and move."

Actually, when Moshe arrived in the acute geriatric unit and the doctors were able to control his diabetes mellitus, the bedsores finally healed, even before he was able to walk.

❖ ❖ ❖ 7 ❖ ❖ ❖

# Stimulation

Is there any efficacy in stimulating comatose patients? A great deal of evidence indicates that infant development requires an environment that stimulates the baby to realize his or her potential. Parents must play with, talk to, handle, demonstrate for, sing, rock, and cuddle the baby. But there seems to be no hard evidence that such stimulation is required to arouse a comatose patient or that it is in any way beneficial to such patients.

Yet it is difficult to do nothing. We kept hearing of unconscious patients whose families had stayed close to them, touched them, talked to them. Some of these people had been rewarded with the restoration of their loved one's consciousness.

Our refusal to dissociate ourselves emotionally from Moshe, combined with our tentative hope that we might bring him back to us by stimulating him, kept alive my sons' and my determination to continue visiting Moshe daily. Some doctors stated bluntly that these visits would fulfill only our own needs. "He is totally unaware of your presence," they insisted. But we all wanted to spare no effort; even if it was more than doubtful that our presence would help Moshe return to the land of the living, we could not afford to leave anything untried. After all, we had nothing to lose and everything to gain.

So despite the discouragement of the doctors, we tried to communicate with Moshe. We told him the news about ourselves and about people he knew. We reported the innumerable phone calls we received from friends and relatives all over the world. We shared with him our warm feelings about friends who supported us by visiting us at home and in the hospital. Jonathan brought his radio cassette player and let Moshe hear classical music through the earphones. Alon prayed with him every evening. Above all, each of us constantly assured Moshe of our love and our belief that he was slowly improving and would ultimately wake up.

It was not difficult for us to relate to Moshe—he only looked as if he were fast asleep. But slowly and imperceptibly my talks to Moshe became less communicative. The first to go were the doubts and quandaries I normally would have shared with him. I did not even hint at my problems and worries and I kept my feelings of hopelessness and despair to myself. I was unwilling to tell him the truth about his condition and how I felt about it. Instead, I now shared all these anxieties with my children.

Almost everyone who tried to communicate with Moshe spoke in a very loud voice. It was as if we felt we had to penetrate a deep fog in order to reach him. A patient in the next bed was the first to draw Alon's attention to the fact that I was shouting to Moshe. The patient felt strongly that Moshe was "present" but unable to communicate. When Alon reported this exchange to me, I tried to lower my voice and asked others to do likewise. But it was not easy for me. I needed much conscious effort not to shout at Moshe—he seemed so far away.

Only a great writer like Virginia Woolf could do full justice to the kind of situation in which I found myself. She depicted such a scene admirably in her early novel *The Voyage Out*. Terence and Rachel have recently become engaged when Rachel becomes extremely ill. Terence visits her regularly at her bedside.

> She did not look very ill. Sitting by her side he would tell her what he had been doing, using his natural voice to speak to her, only a few tones lower down than usual; but by the time he had sat there for five minutes he was plunged in the deepest gloom. She was not the same; he could not bring them back to their old relationship; but although he knew that it was foolish he could not prevent himself from endeavoring to bring her back, to make her remember, and when this failed he was in despair.

# ❖ ❖ ❖ 8 ❖ ❖ ❖
# Glimpses of Improvement

We all watched, hawklike, for the smallest signs of change in Moshe, to counteract the daily discouraging bulletins of "no change" from the nurses. After Alon told us the exciting news that Moshe had opened his right eye on day thirteen, we competed with each other trying to discover further signs of wakefulness. Alon was also the first to notice the tremors in Moshe's right arm after four weeks, soon followed by movement in that arm. Tremors were followed by movement in the right leg a few days later and in the left arm at the end of the sixth week. However, there were no signs of movement in Moshe's left leg. Since that leg had never moved after the first operation—unlike the other three extremities—we were sure it was paralyzed. But meanwhile new movements started: Moshe began to turn his head to the side.

In the eighth week, we could hardly believe our eyes when we noticed slight tremors in Moshe's left leg. None of us mentioned this to the others at first, fearing that it was wishful thinking. But not long thereafter, movements in the left leg became unmistakable. To our joy, our fear that the leg was paralyzed had turned out to be false.

About this time also, Moshe's grip, first with the right hand, then with the left, became stronger. He seemed to respond to our own firm grips. After a few days, his right hand developed a pincerlike grip which was tight enough to cause pain and prevent the other person from removing his or her hand. This was clearly a pathological response, probably related to the spasticity (stiffness) of his right hand muscles. But that Moshe was able to react when someone shook his hand and that he could move his arms and legs indicated progress, however slow. We felt more hopeful.

At this point Dr. Solomon, the physician in charge of the ward, thought it necessary to dampen our enthusiasm. He pointed out to us that it is not sufficient for a professor to be able to respond to a handshake or to move his arms and legs. Moshe would have to give evidence of cognition such as speech to show us he was really progressing. In fact, as we discovered many months later, most doctors did not consider these signs to amount to any significant improvement. Basically they had written Moshe off.

Now we witnessed sudden violent twitchings below Moshe's mouth. When I asked the physiotherapist about this she said simply, "caused by brain damage"—words that cut me like a knife.

In the seventh week, Moshe became able to focus his eyes and to follow moving objects. This state is sometimes known as *coma vigil,* a form of limited responsiveness to the environment. Although almost immobile, Moshe appeared to be alert since his eyes were able to follow visual stimuli. The nurses told us they felt as if someone were watching their every move. To us it looked as if Moshe might speak at any moment.

The doctors, always skeptical of our reports of improvements in Moshe, noticed the new development a week after we had first mentioned it to them. Although they were encouraged, they warned us that it was impossible to know how much more progress Moshe would make.

Moshe still did not respond to commands. He could not open or close his eyes or move any of his limbs on demand. The request that he move a specific part of his body seemed to trigger the movement of other limbs, especially the right arm, which writhed "involuntarily." He appeared to understand the command but seemed unable to carry it out.

Nor did Moshe show the slightest ability to communicate with hand or eye movements. Rodney and his wife, Joni, tried unsuccessfully to make Moshe open and close his eyes to convey yes and no. However, the associated limb movements confused matters so that we were never certain whether Moshe understood the instructions.

I leave the reader to picture my delight when, seven weeks after the operation, Tamara first noticed Moshe bringing his hand up to his face to shoo away a fly that had settled on his chin. We had all grumbled about the flies in the room on the day before the main operation. Now we welcomed these pests as diagnostic aids in testing Moshe's sensitivity to mild stimuli but above all in assessing his ability to perform purposeful actions. It was clear to me that at long last Moshe was displaying movements that could not occur without the involvement of the mind.

## Baby

As Moshe slowly progressed, we could not fail to compare him with our small grandson. It was evident that Elisha at five months was more advanced than his grandfather two months after his surgery. Elisha could smile and relate to people emotionally and vocally. Moshe showed no emotional reactions—his occasional fleeting smiles seemed unrelated to anything in the outside world. Both Elisha and Moshe followed moving objects with their eyes and were able to focus on a person who looked at them, but Moshe did so only rarely; usually he averted his gaze, looking down. Moreover, Elisha was beginning to crawl, while Moshe could not even turn himself in bed.

"Will Moshe's speech start like that of an infant, with babbling?" we asked ourselves. The idea seemed abhorrent to us. After all, this was a man who had mastered numerous Semitic and classical languages as well as several modern ones. At the rate of a toddler's speech development, Moshe could never be expected to regain more than one or at most two languages; to recover a proficiency in many might take him several years. As we posed this question we were not aware that most of the medical profession considered it absolutely impossible that Moshe, after such a prolonged and deep coma, would ever again be able to communicate in any language.

The comparison between Elisha and Moshe was turned into a competition by Moshe many months later. Tamara phoned one day to tell us excitedly that Elisha, aged thirteen months, had just walked unaided halfway across the room. Moshe, on hearing this news, walked into the adjoining room and back without his cane for the first time. He did not want to lag behind his grandson!

# ❖ ❖ ❖ 10 ❖ ❖ ❖
## Keeping Sane

An Amharic proverb says: "Why worry about those on a journey? It is the ones left behind [the relatives] who carry the brunt of the suffering." Moshe, far away from us, did not suffer any pain or anguish. Only his family had to contend with these feelings.

There was no one to ask, nothing to read. Models simply did not exist for family members in a situation that looked desperate, but in which hope had to be kept alive. It was so different from having a close relative with cancer or heart disease. In those more usual cases one knew what to expect from stage to stage: what the suffering was, how it could be alleviated, how the illness might progress, and what its outcome might be. One could consult people who had survived such illnesses themselves or whose relatives, friends, or acquaintances had suffered from them. One could even obtain a straightforward answer from a doctor.

In Moshe's case, no one had any answers. Even the doctors who kept hoping made no predictions about the progress of Moshe's condition.

Lea's husband had been comatose for five weeks after his open-heart surgery and then awakened. She contacted me in the recovery room to encourage me not to lose hope. Everyone warned me that each case is unique. Yet I was full of expectancy when Moshe arrived at week five, in the hope that he would likewise regain consciousness at that time. Alas, it was not to be.

I realized that I had to find the appropriate metaphor by which to live. I wondered if I should think of Moshe as a soldier missing in action. But a missing person is either alive or dead; there is no ambiguity about his state—it is just that his loved ones do not know where he is and in what condition. Moshe's state, however, was intermediate: not really alive and not really dead.

One morning, as I was on my way to the hospital, a metaphor occurred to me: "Moshe has gone on a journey but has not informed us when he will return." Here was both the indeterminate future and my hope for Moshe's return. With this metaphor I lived, waiting for Moshe to come back and envisioning a future together with him.* I kept newspaper clippings I thought would interest him and made lists of the people who had telephoned to inquire about him, with a view to sharing these items with him one day.

I conjured up certain images whenever I wanted to raise my hopes. Both metaphor and images encompassed a future in which Moshe was alive and active. In one image I saw Moshe sitting in his armchair with a group of friends around him. He was telling them about his coma and what he had experienced during that time. In another image I had invited Dr. Benson, Moshe's cardiac surgeon, and Dr. Davies, his anesthesiologist, to dinner with Moshe and me. The medical relationship had been transformed into a social and friendly one. A veritable happy ending!

As for the day-to-day living, the psychologist in me determined soon after Moshe's second operation that life had to continue and that each of us must carry on as normally as possible under the circumstances. This created a schizoid type of existence in which we would spend part of the day at Moshe's bedside and the rest of the day in our regular occupations. I started seeing patients again in week two and tried to run my household as I had done previously. I knew that had Moshe been able to make any decisions, he would have suggested this, especially since we had no idea how long he would be ill. I also

*The fascinating coda to this is that when Moshe did recover full consciousness, he frequently told people with whom he had not been in close contact, like his bank manager, that he had been away on a journey. Only about two months after coming out of the coma did he realize that metaphorically he had been on a journey farther than the moon. He was unaware that he had used the same metaphor I had used to help me survive emotionally.

knew that this way of life required that I insulate my feelings in a soft coat of numbness.

❖

In order to give my best energies to Moshe, I had to look after myself. That meant first and foremost eating properly and getting enough sleep. I always tried to rest when I came home from the hospital at noon so as to be alert for my afternoon patients. But I was exhausted by nine in the evening and regularly fell asleep whenever I tried to relax by watching television or a movie. I woke up very early in the morning and was nervous, jittery, and tearful by the time I had to get up. It was hard for me to face a new day with its unknown ordeals. Yet I had no alternative but to fulfill my duties. For the first time in my life I resorted to tranquilizers, which I continued to use in the mornings during the first month.

I realized that I could not do everything singlehandedly and indulged myself by keeping my part-time household helper. A large part of my day was spent in hospital visits, another block of time invested in my patients. Having a helper meant that my home would not be neglected and that I would have the food and clean clothes I needed.

I made a special effort to remain healthy. I remembered having read about Mrs. Schroeder, whose husband had an artificial heart implanted. Her children's concern about *her* health was said to have added greatly to their stress. They were quoted as saying: "The only thing worse than having one parent in the hospital is having two." Through the first few weeks I suffered from diarrhea and lost eleven pounds. Medication was unable to eliminate the parasites that the laboratory exams revealed. It was obvious to me that my being upset interfered with curing the diarrhea.

I was particularly afraid of catching a cold because it might prevent me from visiting Moshe. Also, I was afraid of passing on an infection to him. I tried to avoid risks of all kinds. I never sat next to a taxi driver (as is legal in Israel)—I knew of too many car accidents in which the person in the right front seat was the most seriously injured.

I tried to minimize stress by relinquishing emotional commitments for which I had formerly volunteered. For instance, I used to visit chronically ill friends and acquaintances who were unable to leave their hospital wards or homes. I felt that I now had to concentrate my time and energy on Moshe and did not have the strength to give to others in need as well. I had to learn to be selfish in a very specific way; since I had less time to call my own, I had to spend whatever was left of the day on people and activities that I found necessary or worthwhile. This meant that some social obligations fell by the wayside.

In order to help boost my morale and also to prevent people from feeling pity for "this miserable-looking woman," I tried to look as good as I could, and went to the hairdresser at least once a week.

To renew myself emotionally, I spent time with close friends, went to movies, and listened to classical music. I indulged myself by taking taxis rather than buses, to save time. I was not able to read books— I simply lacked the concentration. The most I could manage was to leaf through a newspaper or magazine.

I had the good will of most people with whom I came into contact, and I allowed myself to luxuriate in it. Many people went out of their way to help me. For example, our family physician, Dr. Peretz, who works mornings at Hadassah, offered to see me about my diarrhea at his Hadassah office. He instructed the nurse to put me ahead of all the other patients waiting to see him. He must have realized that had he not made these special arrangements, I would have neglected my own health.

People were willing to make allowances for my sins of omission and commission. So I knew, for instance, that I did not have to attend the wedding of the daughter of Moshe's colleague. Yet if I decided to make the extra effort and go to the wedding, I could be sure of a special welcome.

## Family

Moshe is a man who wears several hats. He is a professor of Semitic and Biblical studies with a worldwide reputation—the "master-teacher," as one of his students referred to him. He lectures at Hebrew University and Bar Ilan University and has also taught at Tel Aviv University, Brandeis University, New York University, Yeshiva University, and the Jewish Theological Seminary. He has thrice been invited to spend sabbaticals at Harvard University. He has published hundreds of scholarly articles and more than a dozen books and heads several large scholarly projects.

During Moshe's illness one of his colleagues in the United States wrote to me: "You are married to one of the great minds of our time. Naturally there are a number of first-rate scholars both here and across the ocean but Moshe looks the largest and the most intimidating of them all. What confirms the fact that he belongs among the few world-class scholars in our field is that none of us sees anyone coming along who could be a successor or even do a small part of the things that Moshe has done."

The private Moshe is primarily a family man; yet he is always ready to listen, help, or advise anyone who needs him. He enjoys people and has the talent of communicating in a way that makes the other person feel special.

Moshe is strong-willed, highly critical, and demanding of himself and of others. For this reason, some find him rather formidable. He is dynamic, competitive, and achievement oriented, a typical type A personality. As a counterbalance he has a marvelous sense of humor with a special gift for punning, and he rarely takes himself seriously. He says the most outrageous things to people he knows well, making them burst into laughter.

During Moshe's coma I felt acute loss. I missed the father of my children, the man with whom I shared my daily experiences, some-one with whom I could let down my hair, someone I could consult and whose judgment I respected. I felt that no one knew me half as well as he. I missed my travel companion; I missed the man who laughed with me. As I thought about Moshe's unfinished work, I felt guilty that I had so often diverted him from it for social occasions, which he frequently regarded as a waste of time. Ever since I first knew him, he had believed that he was living on borrowed time because of his predisposition to cardiac disease. With typical gallows humor he would refer to himself as "your late husband" and would speak about his own "untimely death." I became accustomed to his morbid sense of humor and tried to ignore its implications. But he worked like a sick man in a hurry. His conviction that he would one day have cardiac problems was so strong that when we looked for a new apartment—he was then only thirty-five years old—he insisted that it be on the ground floor since he "knew" that he would sooner or later develop cardiac problems and be unable to climb stairs.

Only when he was in the hospital did I learn something of the impact Moshe had on the lives of so many people. Malka, his adoring student, saw to it that special prayers were recited on his behalf. In a broken voice, she told me that Moshe used to shout at her for not doing her work. "How I wish he would shout at me again!" She visited him in the hospital and wiped his brow devotedly.

Moshe often had mock arguments with Shimon, the electrician, about the prices he charged. Shimon was truly upset when he saw Moshe in the hospital. He expressed his appreciation of a man he considered "head and shoulders above other people" who nevertheless "always talked to me."

Barbara, the gardener, wept for half an hour when I told her about Moshe's comatose state. "He is the only one who took time to make me laugh," she said. Barbara had been widowed in her late twenties and had to raise two small children alone. Moshe, with characteristic empathy, provided for her what she most needed: occasions for laughter.

❖

I could rely absolutely on Alon, Tamara, Jonathan, and Yona. I knew they would give unflinchingly of their time and energy, without being asked. They became my fellow participants in the endeavor to return Moshe to the land of the living.

Alon and Jonathan are sensitive, intelligent, insightful men who relate easily to people and have a great sense of humor. Yet they are also very different from each other.

Alon, in his late twenties at the time of Moshe's coma, taught rabbinic thought at Hebrew University. After obtaining his bachelor's degree he studied Jewish texts with his father. Together they had planned Alon's doctoral dissertation on which he was working. Moshe was Alon's most effective critic and adviser, and the two had become very close. Alon would have gone fearlessly to the end of the world to help his father get well.

Alon finds his spiritual base in the world of religion and meditation. He is particularly attracted to Hasidic circles. He devotes several hours daily to prayer and meditation. These practices helped reassure Alon about Moshe's recovery, regardless of the vicissitudes in his condition. Nor was Alon daunted by the dire prognosis of the medical experts; he was confident that however long the illness, Moshe would ultimately return to the land of the living, basically functioning as he had done prior to the operation.

Alon became the pillar of optimism on whom I leaned for support. His strength and belief never wavered. Whenever my despair took the upper hand, I would call him up and cry to him about the hopelessness of Moshe's condition. He would say to me, in the most matter-of-fact way: "But you know that Dad will eventually be well." It was most comforting to be drawn into this total conviction. But at times my doubts were too powerful for such comfort. Then Alon would assume a paradoxical posture: "OK, the doctors are right. Dad will not get better." This sounded so absurd coming out of his mouth that it would make me laugh and realize that only the opposite could be true.

Those of us who knew the reason for Alon's optimism feared for him in case Moshe did not recover. We knew that such an outcome might destroy Alon totally; the loss of his beloved and admired father could also threaten his faith.

I was particularly eager that Alon should complete the doctorate on which his professional future depended. He needed time and concentration for this. Even more important, he needed time to be with Tamara and their little son. So Alon chose the late evening hours for visiting his father, leaving the daytime for his family and his thesis.

Alon's wife, Tamara, is a warm, bright, and helpful person. She not only kept me company with baby Elisha in the hospital garden, but she also telephoned me regularly, trying to bolster my morale. Whenever she sensed that I had reached rock bottom emotionally, she brought Elisha to me. This never failed to cheer me up. The little fellow, unaware of the desperate situation around him, infected me with his smiles and laughter.

❖

Jonathan, twenty-five years old at the time of Moshe's hospitalization, is also a strictly observant Jew but has a more skeptical disposition than his older brother. A proponent of the scientific method, he did not easily give credence to reports of apparent improvement in Moshe, dependent as they were on observer error. It was far more difficult to convince Jonathan of Moshe's progress than it was to assure Alon, in whom wishful thinking frequently predominated. No wonder Jonathan was often depressed and on the verge of despair. Occasionally his emotions made him ill, and he was compelled to take time out from hospital visits. Thus, the two men balanced each other's attitudes and feelings: Alon, the optimist, Jonathan, the skeptic. I seemed to take the center position, since I wavered between hopefulness and despair.

I wanted Jonathan to complete the psychology studies in which he had done so brilliantly during the first two years. The time for his annual examinations approached. I knew his mind was not on his studies, but I earnestly entreated him to prepare himself for the exams. He did so, largely in response to my urging, although he admitted it was a kind of occupational therapy for him. He had no time to read the required literature in experimental psychology, his forte. When he finished the exam he did not even want to discuss it with his fellow students. But when the results came, Jonathan got a 93; most of the class got marks in the 70s. Here was one thing at last that really made him feel good.

Jonathan also needed time to be with Yona, who was a great support to him in those dark weeks. She had gone with him into the recovery room the first few times, and they had cried together afterward. Jonathan had introduced her to us shortly before Moshe's hospitalization. We were struck by her maturity, sensitivity, tact, and intelligence. Jonathan and she had visited Moshe at Shaare Zedek Hospital when Moshe had his angina attacks. Moshe had been happy to see how well suited they seemed to each other. I wanted Jonathan to enjoy his courtship as much as he could under the troubled circumstances.

Jonathan became my chief physical support after Moshe's operation. He insisted that I eat properly, bringing iced coffee to the waiting room and buying me French baguettes to stimulate my appetite. He arranged for friends and family members to be at my side during the long hours of waiting in the hospital. He even contacted my friend

Adena at eleven one night. She had arrived from Philadelphia the previous evening—two days after Moshe's operation—on a visit to Jerusalem; Jonathan asked her to come to see me at once. Adena came, and we talked and talked until Jonathan knocked on the door to remind Adena that I needed rest. I was greatly touched by Jonathan's concern for me but explained that I was quite capable of determining my own bedtime.

Similarly, when he tried to make sure that I never went to the hospital alone, I reminded him that I had been an independent adult before this tragedy occurred and was not about to become a dependent child as a result of it; in fact, I did not mind being on my own. I felt that this statement of my position gave Jonathan the freedom to live a life of his own without the additional stress of worrying about me. He did voluntarily assume some of Moshe's duties, such as handling money matters and repairing things around the house.

❖

My mother, my sister Rita, and my brother Leo called almost daily from London. They tried to support me, but since I knew they were waiting to hear about signs of improvement in Moshe, I felt as if I was letting them down. After the third day, I noticed that these calls were depressing me. Yet I felt obliged to keep my London family up to date. Alon jumped into the fray and offered to talk to my mother, suggesting that she call him rather than me in the future. She was rewarded by his optimistic descriptions of Moshe's condition, which he totally believed.

My brother Gershon called me from Los Angeles for a daily medical bulletin. In order to get a clearer picture of the situation he also phoned Rodney several times. With the facts thus obtained, he inquired among his colleagues in the fields of medicine pertinent to Moshe's condition. He then phoned to encourage me, highlighting at each point those facts that he considered positive for Moshe's prognosis. He pointed out to me that Moshe's continuing progress, although slow, could be charted on a graph. About two months after Moshe's surgery, Gershon claimed that Moshe had a 50 percent chance of recovery. Even thousands of miles away, he gave me more hope than the doctors who saw Moshe. Perhaps the fact that Gershon did not see Moshe enabled him to be more confident.

Both my mother and Gershon's wife, Linda, offered to fly to Israel to be with me. I gratefully declined their offers, since I was trying to lead as normal a life as possible. Their appearance would have signified for me that things were falling apart at the seams to such an extent that I needed help in coping with daily life.

## Friends

I received phone calls 'round the clock from people in Israel and abroad. These calls were very important to me: they enabled me to tell the story of traumatic events repeatedly and also to obtain support. I kept the phone next to my bed so that I could take calls at night from abroad.

During the first few weeks after Moshe's operation I functioned like a telephone answering service. I arranged to see my patients at times when I thought people were less likely to phone—in the middle of the day. I felt a kind of obligation to transmit good news to the callers, many of whom sounded distressed. Slowly it dawned on me that I did not have to supply a service for anyone and that, in fact, the calls were mainly intended for my benefit. Once that became clear to me, I saw patients when it suited me best. My friends and relatives quickly learned to phone at my convenience.

A large informal network developed in which certain people were phoned for information about Moshe's condition. Not everyone felt close enough to disturb me. Nor did I have enough time to answer the phone since I was at the hospital for several hours every day. Alon; my uncle Werner; Moshe's chief assistant, Shraga; my cousin Itamar; my friend Hilda; one of Moshe's closest colleagues and friends, Jonas; our friend Marvin in Boston; and my mother in London all served as resources for the latest knowledge about Moshe.

Some friends from abroad could not afford to phone me regularly. Many of them wrote me encouraging letters full of sympathy and love. In those dark and gloomy days they kept up my courage.

I made a point of answering most of the letters since I wanted to stay in contact with these friends and knew that I could not expect to receive without giving. Also, answering letters was a form of catharsis for me, permitting me not only to tell my story of catastrophe to those who cared but also to share with them any hopeful signs, however small they might be.

Many friends appeared in person, to hug me and to hear the latest reports about Moshe. The sheer number of these visitors, like the numerous phone calls, helped me to realize how truly dreadful Moshe's condition was. These unannounced visitors resembled people coming to visit mourners. This association was reinforced when Shlomo, an old acquaintance, dropped in to see me. I inquired about his wife and was told that she was about to go to a wedding and felt she was dressed inappropriately to visit me. Apparently she felt she had to wear black.

Friends repeatedly asked, "How can I help you?" My spontaneous response was: "I wish there were something you could do to make Moshe recover consciousness." But some friends offered practical assistance, like driving me to the hospital (I had given up driving a few years earlier) or inviting me to dinner or doing my shopping. It took me a while to realize that although I could afford to pay for taxis, it was infinitely more pleasant to be driven by my friends. I even realized that I was doing these friends a favor by accepting their offers, permitting them to help in some concrete way. Likewise, when Moshe needed twenty-three pints of blood, his colleagues and friends and Jonathan's former classmates at *yeshiva* rushed to the blood bank; this helped them feel that they were actively contributing to Moshe's recovery.

Few friends visited Moshe unaccompanied. Usually they brought their marriage partners or one of Moshe's colleagues, presumably for support. Many friends and colleagues could not bring themselves to visit Moshe in the hospital at all. They seemed unable to face seeing him in a vegetative state—although several of them later told me that if I had asked them to visit Moshe, they would not have refused. Even though they did not visit Moshe, I knew that they cared, for they called me or came to see me at home in order to express their feelings.

For the first few weekends I accepted invitations from friends for the Sabbath dinner. I was always warmly welcomed on those occasions, although I tended to doze off at the end of the meal. Eventually

I decided that I had to stop living like a nomad. This decision propelled me to return to a more normal way of life in which I prepared Sabbath meals to which I invited my children and friends, as I had done when Moshe was well. I occasionally went out for dinner with people I liked, but I no longer made a habit of it. I felt I could cope independently.

My friends Kyrstyna and Pnina had gone through similar traumas, their husbands having been extremely ill. They seemed like kindred spirits who had real inside knowledge of what I was experiencing. Pnina knew from first-hand experience that neurologists' predictions were not necessarily correct. Her husband had been operated on for the removal of a brain tumor. The doctors had predicted that his personality would completely change and that he would live no longer than six weeks. Yet his personality remained unchanged and he lived for five and a half very productive years, in which he wrote his most important books.

The people who visited Moshe regularly, who kept me company in moments of crisis, or who drove me to the hospital or invited me to their homes are too numerous to be named here. But I remember with special gratitude those who, when they visited Moshe, pointed out signs of improvement and transmitted their hopefulness to me.

Usually a friend's or relative's first visit would depress me. In the expression and demeanor of such a "novice" I would discern shock at seeing Moshe lying helpless in bed and unable to react to anyone —a state to which I had become accustomed by degrees. I dreaded most particularly my mother's first hospital visit. She flew in from London three months after Moshe's surgery. Jonathan volunteered to accompany her to the hospital, thereby sparing me anguish.

Some people I shall always remember for their exceptional acts of kindness. Outstanding among these was Shraga, Moshe's former student and now his teaching and research assistant. He spent many hours daily in the waiting room and was the first non-medical, non-family member to see Moshe in the recovery room. No son could have done more for Moshe. Shraga was distraught during those initial weeks, eager to help us. He was delighted when Alon mislaid his car key and needed Shraga to drive him home. In the ward, Shraga visited Moshe almost daily.

My friend Hilda and my uncle Werner both canceled their summer holidays. Each said the same thing: "How could I enjoy vacationing so far away from you, where I could not find out at any moment what's happening with Moshe?" I could not prevail on either of them to go ahead with their plans.

Hadassah Hospital is far from the center of Jerusalem and we do not travel on the Sabbath. Miriam and Dan, two young dental students, though virtual strangers, invited the family to stay with them in their student apartment next to the hospital for the weekend. During the first Sabbath, Miriam provided three three-course meals for all five of us. Every Sabbath thereafter for the following nine weeks they arranged lodging for us in their own apartment or in a friend's apartment. (It was usually Alon, Tamara, and the baby who spent the Sabbath there.) When I thanked them, Miriam explained that loving kindness had been extended to them in the past and they were happy to repay it now, even though the cast of characters had changed.

Our neighbors Tamar and Simcha implored me to let them do my food shopping. Although I knew they were busy people, I gratefully accepted their offer, expecting them to have the order sent to me. Instead they arrived at my doorstep one morning with the food I had asked them to buy. After they deposited the box on my kitchen table, Tamar shared some glad tidings with me: during the night their first granddaughter had been born in Rehovot, about fifty miles away. They were now going to drive there, to make her acquaintance. I was deeply touched that they had looked after me before attending to their own joyous occasion.

My friends Shirley and Bill invited me over for a specially prepared fish dinner every week, knowing that I do not eat meat. They never forgot to ask me to their home whenever they had other guests they thought I would like, so that I might be distracted for a few hours. They also visited Moshe every week—Bill insisted on driving me to the hospital on each such occasion.

Yona and her sister, Nehama, walked for two hours to the Shaare Zedek Medical Center on Rosh Hashanah, when travel is not allowed, in order to keep Moshe company even though he was in a coma. I hardly knew Nehama at that time, and she did not know Moshe at all. It seemed that Jonathan was going to have not only a wonderful wife but also a sterling sister-in-law.

Of the numerous friends in Boston, Los Angeles, New York, New Haven, London, and Oxford who called me to inquire about Moshe and to encourage me, June and Marvin will always have a special place in my memory. They phoned from Boston once or twice a week, and when they came to Jerusalem for two weeks they visited Moshe several times in the hospital and spent much of their brief stay with me and the family in order to discuss the implications of Moshe's condition and to offer their counsel and material help. As Shakespeare wrote in *Hamlet*:

> The friends thou hast, and their adoption tried,
> Grapple them to thy soul with hoops of steel.

Moshe's condition was the litmus paper that tested the quality of people's humanity. To two of my colleagues I poured out my heart very soon after Moshe's operation. Since both are active in the field of mental health, I expected more than a few routine words of sympathy. But neither so much as called me once during his illness to find out how Moshe was progressing or to ask whether they could assist me in any way.

## Tears

I cried a lot when I was alone. I was not even embarrassed to find myself crying among strangers or at a hospital pay phone or in the corridor outside Moshe's room. After all, I did not know the people in those surroundings, so why should I care if they saw me crying? At times it was more important for me to release some of the pent-up feelings of pain and anguish. Surely, tears are God's very own invention.

I tried not to break down in public with people I knew. For this reason, I did not attend the session of the World Congress of Jewish Studies at which, after the chairman's invocation for Moshe's recovery, Alon read the paper Moshe had written when he was in the intensive coronary unit at Shaare Zedek, before his bypass operation. It was clear to me that if I attended such a meeting I would break down and weep uncontrollably. I aimed for self-control with Moshe's colleagues and former students and I was prepared to share my true feelings only with close friends and family. Above all, I trusted my children most and felt most comfortable in their company.

Yet it was frequently difficult for me to act according to my own principles. Certain conditions caused me to weep irrespective of the environment in which I found myself. Any changes in Moshe's surroundings upset me, especially when he was moved from one department to another.

Moshe's move to the cardiac surgery ward from the recovery room put him with patients healthier than himself. The others were all conscious, talking, eating, and beginning to move around. They never stayed longer than a week or two in the ward. "This is how it could have been and should be," I thought wretchedly when I entered this new ward, and immediately I burst into a flood of tears. The nursing orderly, a simple soul, brought me tea and homemade cakes, imploring me not to cry. But why shouldn't I have cried? Isn't that the most natural reaction to what I faced?

Telling someone who had not heard of Moshe's tragedy what had befallen him made me burst into tears—whether or not I knew the person well. It happened at the hairdresser's or in the department store. I was simply unable to hold back my tears.

Once, reading in a letter from a close friend that "a calamity has befallen the family," seeing it labeled in these terms produced tears. So did the compliments I received about the way I was coping under the circumstances.

On Tisha be'Av, the day of mourning commemorating the destruction of the First Temple in 586 B.C.E. and of the Second Temple in 70 C.E., Alon and I were at Moshe's bedside in the cardiac surgery ward. Alon read to Moshe from the Book of Lamentations, as is customary on that evening. I wept uncontrollably, seeing Moshe's destruction in front of my eyes. I felt the lamentations were for him.

❖

I was often tempted to "tell all" whenever I met an old acquaintance. Two months after Moshe's surgery I decided to attend a psychotherapy symposium. Many of my colleagues were present. During the coffee break I got together with several of them and in reply to a simple "How are you?" I started spilling out the tale of Moshe's illness. I received a great deal of sympathy and understanding. But after I had repeated my story for the third time, I asked myself whether it was proper to use this forum to spread my bad news to whoever would listen. After all, these colleagues had come to devote themselves to a specific topic in psychotherapy. Why did I have to jolt them emotionally by sharing my story with them? Such self-indulgence, I decided, was unnecessary. I was happy that I had made such a resolution and that I was able to carry it through.

## Work

It was vital that I resume my professional activities as soon as I learned that Moshe was in a coma of unpredictable duration. I knew that work was important for my own mental equilibrium.

I had informed my patients that I would not be taking my summer vacation as originally planned since my husband would have to undergo surgery. Most of them had expressed their good wishes for him at the time. When I resumed work a week after Moshe's operation, a few patients showed genuine concern about the outcome of the surgery. Shimon, a doctor who worked at Hadassah Hospital, saw me in the waiting room the day after the second operation and asked whether he could do anything for me. This was a reversal of our usual roles, but under the circumstances I asked him to take a look at Moshe, whom he did not know. He offered me the key to his room at the hospital so that I could rest between visits. I appreciated his compassion but declined his offer. I phoned him a week later to inform him that I was resuming work. In my office he wondered if I could really deal with his problems, which must seem minor in comparison with my own. I assured him that I would try to give him my full attention—after all, life had to continue and with it my work. My assurance enabled him to talk about himself as freely as he had done before Moshe's coma.

Paula was a former patient who was now a nurse at Hadassah.

When she heard about Moshe's condition, she came to see me in the recovery room, where she hugged and comforted me. She used many opportunities to see me and to visit Moshe (whom she had not known). She told me that no illness of any of her relatives or friends had ever affected her so deeply.

But most of my patients either did not ask about Moshe's health or asked only as a polite formality. I would answer vaguely, "There is still room for improvement," after which they concentrated on their own troubles. After all, it was for their problems that they came to see me, not in order to hear about mine. And in the type of therapy I conduct, details of the therapist's life are usually not shared with patients.

One patient's problems interacted curiously with my own. Minna doubted that she could be helped by therapy. I tried to reassure her, but she fought me angrily: how dare I hope that she would improve when she was so sure that she would not? She seemed to want to protect herself from disappointment by denying herself hope. But for me the problem of sustaining hope at a time when things appeared at their worst was crucial. By becoming her champion for hope, I also became my own champion for a concept in which I needed to believe.

Several weeks after Moshe's operation a new patient, Annabelle, told me that her mother was about to have similar surgery. She turned to me and asked: "Do you know what a bypass is?" I was tempted to reply, "You must be joking!" Annabelle wanted me to help her face the possibility of her mother's death. "Little does she realize that there are fates worse than death," I thought. Of course we did work on her problems related to her mother's surgery, and I communicated to her neither my own thoughts and concerns nor any of the events relating to Moshe's surgery.

"The distress of many is distress halved" is a Hebrew proverb. Those seeking help supplied clear evidence that I was not the only one in the world who suffered. But it was more important to me that I was able to be of help to my patients—in contrast to the situation with Moshe, in which I felt totally helpless. Moreover, when I was concentrating on their problems, I was usually able to forget my own misery.

❖ ❖ ❖ 11 ❖ ❖ ❖

# Meaning

Why did this terrible catastrophe befall Moshe? The question haunted me day and night. Of course I knew rationally that any number of complications could result from major surgery. But how many patients (if you exclude those who have brain surgery) remain in a deep coma? Certainly only a tiny fraction. Why did Moshe have to be among these exceptional few? I knew that this question is asked by everyone afflicted by life-threatening calamities: "Why my child; why my marriage partner; why me?"

There are no ready answers. But in times of deep crisis, those who believe in God have a definite advantage. It seemed to me that Alon perceived this dreadful disaster as a trial by God. Here was a neat reversal: an awful tribulation turned into the privilege of the chosen few. But surely this way of understanding what had befallen Moshe raised more questions than it answered. Why was Moshe considered especially worthy of God's love and therefore in need of being tested by Him? And was it really Moshe, the unconscious patient, undergoing the ordeal, or was it those nearest to him, who were fully aware of what was happening? Suppose *we* were the objects of God's trial. Why then were *we* being tested in this way? What was our special merit or fault that we deserved such exceptional treatment? To me it smacked of hubris to imagine that God had singled out Moshe and our family for such terrible and extraordinary trials.

If God was to be implicated at all it looked to me as if He were laughing at all of us by reversing everything. We were faced with the irony that a man who was all mind had been transformed into a man who was seemingly mindless. Was God demonstrating to us that there is no certainty in this life? Suddenly, in less than no time, anything can happen: presence can turn into absence.

But it seemed even more plausible to me that, if there is a God, He has nothing to do with the fate of individual people. In other words, I saw no meaning in Moshe's appalling condition. It had merely occurred, without any reason or purpose.

However, I did feel that this was my great test. Irrespective of a divinity, I had to prove myself to myself in the face of terrible adversity. I was both the agent and the judge of my own behavior. I set myself certain aims which I tried to fulfill. I had to remain strong to be a support and model for my children. I had to keep coping with life, even when the temptation was to surrender entirely to pain and grief.

❖  ❖  ❖ 12 ❖  ❖  ❖

## Penultimate Stop

Eight weeks after Moshe's surgery, Dr. Benson concluded that Moshe needed a different kind of care than the cardiac surgery ward at Hadassah could provide for him. Moshe's problems no longer had to do with cardiac surgery; he would be better off in the chronic geriatric unit of Shaare Zedek.

Dr. Benson called Alon, Jonathan, and me together. He tried to sweeten the pill by telling us how impressed he and his staff were with the way we had conducted ourselves in this terrible crisis. Before my mind's eye there appeared a framed certificate of praise, signed by Dr. Benson, hanging above my bed. How unfortunate that such a certificate could do nothing for any of us! After all, the point of it all was not to impress the hospital staff but to provide Moshe with the best physical facilities so as to enable him to recover as quickly as possible.

After sharing his views with us, Dr. Benson called in the geriatric specialist of Shaare Zedek Medical Center, Dr. Reisman, for a consultation. Dr. Reisman agreed to take Moshe into his chronic unit as soon as there was an empty bed.

Alon was present at this consultation. He demonstrated to both physicians that when he said "Open your mouth" to Moshe, Moshe seemed to respond, enabling Alon to wet his lips with a gauze-covered stick. But Dr. Reisman wondered whether Moshe had really reacted to Alon's verbal request. He thought that Moshe had opened his mouth when he sensed the stick on his lips.

In times of great stress, events often seem symbolic. On the day Dr. Benson told us that Moshe would be transferred, my watch stopped. My first reaction was, "Oh God, this is the end." But I did not allow myself to think these defeatist thoughts for long. Instead, I went to the watchmaker, who exchanged the battery, whereupon the watch functioned as accurately as before. So maybe Moshe would have a new lease on life as well.

The chronic geriatric unit provides long-term nursing care. Its human scenery is grim: elderly people tied to their wheelchairs sit in the corridor. One screams incessantly, another rocks ceaselessly. Only a few patients talk to one another or to visitors. Most of them merely sit staring ahead of them or sleep. The more seriously ill patients lie in their rooms.

So this would be Moshe's next stop! I broke down when I saw his future fellow patients. I had never thought of him as either incurably ill or old. Mrs. Nathan, the administrator, tried to comfort me: "After all, your husband is unaware of his surroundings. As soon as he becomes aware of them, he'll leave for the rehabilitation unit. It is not he who will suffer but his family." I realized that, whenever I had reached what I considered to be my full share of misery, I had to stretch a little more and endure even greater pain. I would just have to grit my teeth and bear it.

I remembered a similar emotionally escalating circumstance. During the 1973 Yom Kippur War, I, like many other mental health practitioners, volunteered to visit families who had lost a husband or father or son on active duty. Most of those visits were painful; apart from the grief and sorrow that we both witnessed and experienced, the volunteers were blamed by families who perceived us as representatives of the administration and therefore as responsible for the tragedy that had befallen them. But there was an even more difficult duty that had to be performed: accompanying an army officer to announce a death to the family. I decided to take on this additional task after I had worked for a few weeks with bereaved families. So I shouldered even greater pain.

It is fortunate that human beings are creatures of habit. After a while, they become used to any situation, however terrible it may be. Pnina told of visiting her critically ill husband in the hospital every day for many weeks. After he died she continued for a time to drive daily to the hospital, simply because it had become a habit for her and she could not easily relinquish it.

Knowledgeable friends confirmed that the chronic geriatric unit was the best of its kind in Jerusalem, with a most devoted staff. Yet the decision to transfer Moshe there was a particularly hard one, and I kept putting it off. One evening Yona's father Yossi called me up. A senior physician in Shaare Zedek Medical Center, he had pulled many strings to make sure that the first empty bed in the chronic geriatric unit would be made available to Moshe. He realized that giving consent for Moshe's transfer to this unit was a very difficult step for me. But as the head of the family I would have to act soon; otherwise the bed might be given to another patient.

Bayla, a psychiatrist friend, accompanied me to the unit for another close look before I made up my mind. She pointed out how well taken care of the patients seemed. This was, after all, my primary concern. So I finally gave my consent for Moshe's transfer as soon as a bed became available. I felt I had no other option.

On Monday morning, exactly ten weeks after Moshe's surgery, I was called at 9:15 A.M. by a nurse from the cardiac surgery unit. I was in the middle of a session with a patient. The nurse informed me that the ambulance would pick up Moshe in an hour's time to take him to Shaare Zedek. Vainly I pleaded for an hour's delay. The phone call had caught me totally unprepared. I had expected to be given a little more notice.

I had no choice but to send my patient home early—the first time in my professional life that I had done such a thing.

Moshe arrived at Shaare Zedek not one minute too soon. Had he been late, the bed would have been given to another patient. Moshe was assigned to a room with two extremely sick old men. The male nursing orderly assigned to him looked incredulous when I told him that Moshe was a professor. He asked whether Moshe was my father. I felt that I had reached rock bottom.

Other problems awaited us. Edith, the head nurse, was horrified to see Moshe and did not even want to meet me. She complained that she had too many seriously ill patients in her unit and too few nurses and orderlies to look after them. She had been away for several weeks and thus had not been consulted regarding Moshe's admission. She now absolutely refused to admit Moshe to her ward unless one of the other seriously ill patients were transferred to a different ward. Edith, Mrs. Nathan, and Yossi argued for several hours. Finally Mrs. Nathan called the head of the medical center for advice. He examined Moshe and agreed to Mrs. Nathan's suggestion that Dr. Reisman, the geriatrician, be asked to take Moshe into the acute geriatric ward for two weeks in order to stabilize his medical condition. Moshe still had uncontrolled diabetes, and his bedsores had not healed. At the end of this fortnight, Edith promised to care for Moshe in the chronic ward. Dr. Reisman concurred in this arrangement.

It was far from easy for me to witness this argument, although Mrs. Nathan repeatedly assured me that Edith was acting out of concern that her patients get the best possible care.

Moshe was transferred to the acute ward the following morning. Here he had a room to himself (later another patient shared the room). Of course, Moshe could no more enjoy this relative privacy than he could feel upset by the crowding on the chronic ward. However, I felt much better in this setting, which not only was more intimate but also did not have such an obviously disturbed elderly population. Moreover, its staff included more doctors and trained nurses.

Dr. Scheinfeld, a senior physician in the acute geriatric ward, was willing to talk to me after having given Moshe a thorough examination. As we stood at the open door of Moshe's room, I mentioned that I considered Shaare Zedek a transitional hospital for Moshe until he was well enough to go to the rehabilitation center.

"Don't expect him ever to be able to leave this place," was his response.

I told him I knew of a patient similar to Moshe in London who had fully recovered.

"Why do people always quote cases living in Canada, South Africa, England, or other faraway places to me?" he protested.

"Don't take away my hope," I pleaded. "I cannot help Moshe unless I have hope that he'll improve."

"Why, oh why, do the doctors at Hadassah always give the families of patients hope?" he asked in desperation. "It is *we* who then have to disillusion them."

I was glad that I did not break down in his presence. After all, we were standing in a public place. (I had not even been offered a seat in a doctor's office with the door closed.) But I cried when I got home and also on the phone to Alon. He was reassuring: "Nothing new has happened to Dad to make the prognosis worse. The only new element is the doctor who did not previously know him. He has not observed Dad's slow progress as we have done. He can describe only the present findings—he cannot know about the future."

Later my brother Gershon expressed the same opinion: "You sounded most depressed on the phone because of the gloomy prognosis that the geriatrician at Shaare Zedek had given you," he wrote on September 5. "From my vantage point 9,000 miles away, things look different. I can only say that Moshe has clearly been improving week by week, and to say that he has come to the end of the road when each week shows further improvement seems to me to be a nonsensical point of view. I hope that I am right, because it is futile holding out vain hope. However, miracles do happen in medicine, and Moshe's complete recovery would not be the first in a case like this. So keep hoping, and I am encouraged to believe that such a hope will not be misplaced."

A few days later, we asked Dr. Reisman to recommend more physiotherapy for Moshe in order to prevent further deterioration of the muscles. He told us that he doubted Moshe would ever be able to walk again. In fact, he warned us, too much physiotherapy could lead to fractured bones, since Moshe was likely to develop osteoporosis (abnormal porousness and fragility of the bones). We felt that as long as Moshe's mental capacity returned we could accept his remaining in a wheelchair. But of course Dr. Reisman held out no promise that Moshe's mind would ever function again either.

In the elevator, feeling quite wretched, I turned to Alon. "Isn't it time you became less of an optimist and more of a realist? After all, here are two senior physicians, both more than doubtful that Dad will ever recover his mental faculties." Alon merely laughed in response.

While in the acute geriatric ward Moshe had his sixtieth birthday. Before he became ill, I had planned a party for family, friends, and colleagues at which Moshe would be presented with a festschrift to which his former students had contributed. Few are the teachers who have produced so many students able to contribute to scholarship! Now my cousin Itamar called to ask if I wanted to celebrate Moshe's birthday without him. I absolutely did not want to stage Hamlet without the Prince of Denmark.

On September 6 we told Moshe it was his birthday. Shraga brought him flowers. But Moshe remained totally unaware of the date and its importance for him. We vowed to have a belated birthday celebration when Moshe recovered full consciousness. I tried not to think about the birthday in order to spare myself unnecessary pain.

# ❖ ❖ ❖ 13 ❖ ❖ ❖
## Projections

Since the status of Moshe's illness was medically uncertain, several visitors interpreted the situation by projecting their own feelings, needs, and attitudes into it.

Boaz, a former student who had lived abroad for many years, visited Moshe eleven weeks after the operation. Although Boaz tried desperately to make Moshe read and repeat some letters of the alphabet, Moshe did not react to him at all. At this point, Moshe sat with his eyes focused on the other person at least part of the time, so it seemed reasonable to suppose that he could follow instructions.

Boaz had a simple explanation for Moshe's non-compliance with his requests: "He doesn't react to me because he is angry that I did not visit him earlier." It was obvious that Boaz felt guilty for having postponed an anxiety-provoking experience. When he finally gathered the courage to visit Moshe, he was more centered on his own feelings than on Moshe's illness. Had he thought about the nature of

Moshe's condition, he would probably have come up with a different explanation.

Shoshana, a gentle, shy woman, for ten weeks avoided visiting Moshe, leaving the task to her husband, Moshe's colleague and friend, although both of them visited me often. When she came to see Moshe in the geriatric ward and was not rewarded by any kind of reaction from him, she "knew" the reason: "He does not want any women around." Shoshana seemed unaware that Moshe was probably not conscious enough to tell the difference between male and female visitors, much less to express a preference. Probably she feels more comfortable with people of her own sex when ill and presumed that Moshe had similar inclinations.

Ruth visited Moshe three months after the operation. Jonathan had just announced his engagement, and she congratulated Moshe. She reported to me later that Moshe had tried to convey to her that he knew what marriage was about, including its sexual aspects. All this she had deduced from the fact that Moshe had played with his condom catheter (a rubber tube attached to the genital leading to a bag for storing urine). Ruth did not realize that Moshe was constantly playing with the condom catheter and trying to pull it off, just as he tried to pull out the nasogastric tube. She had probably embarked on her own free associations linked to the topic of Jonathan's impending marriage.

Several people close to Moshe had often doubted whether he really liked them. When Moshe did not react to their conversation or look at them, they regarded this as a clear indication that he did not want to have any dealings with them. They felt rejected by him, completely ignoring the fact that Moshe was in a coma.

# ❖ ❖ ❖ 14 ❖ ❖ ❖
## Speech

Six weeks after his surgery Moshe started to emit high vocal sounds. We interpreted these tentatively as groans, a reaction to pain or displeasure; maybe the beginning of some form of communication. We held our breath expectantly.

About a week later the sounds changed from high to low. Now there was no mistaking their nature: they really were groans.

At this time also, we noticed the movements of Moshe's lips. He started whispering nonsense syllables and words that did not belong to any recognizable language. We were thrilled that a man who knew a dozen languages or more could make vocal sounds! Occasionally we discerned some real unvoiced words, like "hand," "ima" (Hebrew for mother), and "good." At least Moshe was not going to babble like a baby. What a relief for all of us! About ten days later (eight weeks after surgery) Anni and Latzi, friends from Tel Aviv, came to visit Moshe. They stood by his bed and talked to him after introducing themselves to him by name. We were all overjoyed when Moshe clearly repeated "Latzi" as if he recognized him. This was the first time he had addressed anyone by name.

Three days later Moshe said "water," "mayim" (Hebrew for water), and "I want to eat." Here was the first indication that he had not lost the ability to form sentences. That week and the following, each of us thought we heard some words, which we repeated back to Moshe both as a reinforcement and as an attempt to check whether we had heard him correctly. But we were never certain that he had actually uttered these words. None of us believed the words had really been formed unless someone else heard them as well. Jonathan and I were particularly skeptical when Alon reported any new words; he was, after all, known to be an incorrigible optimist.

The nurses now started to report to us that Moshe seemed to say something when he was washed and changed in the mornings. However, they were never able to recapture what he had actually said. It was so frustrating! But at least the period in which they repeated "no change" every morning was over.

It was appealing to watch Moshe's return to the living. I hardly dared admit this feeling even to myself, much less to others. I thought of Odysseus coming back from his long wanderings, Orpheus returning from the underworld. At the same time Alon also admitted that he felt privileged to witness Moshe's rebirth. My own joy was, of course, mingled with the constant fear that Moshe might not be fully restored to us, that there would never be a happy end. Nor could I prevent myself from worrying about the slow pace at which this rebirth was taking place. It might take months and even years. That was a terrifying prospect.

I had heard that people coming out of coma speak in the first language they learned, regardless of the language they were most often speaking just before they became unconscious. I had therefore been persuaded to speak to Moshe in German, our mother tongue, throughout this period. I felt a little self-conscious talking in German to him in front of the others in the ward, and so I used to revert to English, the language in which we spoke to each other most frequently (though we always threw in a good sprinkling of German). We both spoke Hebrew at work and with friends.

English is an accepted language in Israel; in fact it has great prestige. German is different. I still carry memories of my life in England during World War II. At that time German was regarded as the enemy's tongue and we were actively discouraged from speaking German in public places.

When Moshe began to speak, the language he used predominantly was German. Thus, ten weeks after the operation, he whispered whole sentences or parts of them: "Was sich da tut!" (What's happening there!), "viel zu schnell" (much too fast), "Ich wundere mich nicht" (I am not surprised). None of what he said made sense in context. He also uttered phrases in Hebrew from the daily prayers, like "He maketh peace in the Heavens."

My sons were happy that they had learned German, although neither of them is fluent in it. Their knowledge of German enabled them to understand Moshe's words and to react appropriately. When

Moshe uttered "Apfelsaft" (apple juice) during his last week in Hadassah, Alon hunted high and low for the commodity. He was eager to reinforce Moshe's will to speak by honoring his request.

Whenever one of us thought we had identified a word, phrase, or sentence correctly, we voiced it for Moshe, who then tended to shout it back. So his voice was functional!

Undefinable sounds accompanied Moshe's incipient speech about ten weeks after his coronary bypass. We feared that something was wrong with his breathing, but we were reassured by the doctors that these noises did not result from any malfunction of his respiratory system. As Moshe spoke more, he uttered more of these superfluous sounds. Birdlike noises, for example, seemed to herald a loss of words.

The three of us were puzzled by Moshe's constant counting in German, starting eleven weeks after the operation. From 45, 46, 47 he might skip to 58 and continue. I felt he was trying to reassure himself that he still remembered his numbers.

There was more exciting news at this time. I said one day, "I'm going." Moshe responded, "She's going." He was using transformational grammar appropriately, a definite sign of reaction and cognitive ability.

Twelve weeks after the operation Moshe seemed to regress; he hardly talked at all. I became depressed and had to be reminded by family and friends that progress is not always linear. Then came an outstanding development: one of our neighbors visited Moshe and introduced himself by his first name, Simcha. Moshe added his surname: "Landau." Simcha, beside himself with excitement, rushed home to share the good news with us.

During the same week, Moshe gave a clear sign that he recognized me, calling me by my name. How I had prayed for this recognition! And when my friend Batya visited him, he said "Esther," which I interpreted as showing that he recognized Batya's association with me.

Moshe's whisperings increased greatly at this time, and he began to utter fairly long German sentences the week thereafter. "Hab' noch was zu Haus zu erzählen" (Have something else to tell at home), "ich hab' zwei Stunden geredet" (I spoke for two hours), "ich hab' recht"

(I am right), "ich bitte abwarten" (I want you to wait), "bitte lass sein" (please leave it), "ich bin bereit zu reisen" (I am prepared to travel), "Ich bin erleichtert, hab' ich gesagt" (I am relieved, I said), "was such' ich hier?" (What am I doing here?), "ich bin ja was. Ich bin ein Doktor" (I am somebody. I am a doctor), "ich hab' vor langer Zeit gesagt" (I said a long time ago), "ich hab' keine Sprechstunde" (I don't have visiting hours), "ich hab' gesagt das geht nicht" (I said that is not possible), "ich versteh' nichts" (I don't understand anything), "ich muss liegen" (I have to lie).

Most of what Moshe said was not in reaction to outside events. But perhaps his declaration that he understood nothing referred to what was happening to him; perhaps "I have to lie" referred to lying in bed; perhaps he wondered why he was in the hospital. Perhaps, also, he was making a statement that he is a "somebody", that is to say, a doctor (though not one who sees patients in his office) when he declared: "Ich habe keine Sprechstunde." All the sentences were in the first person singular and sounded grammatically and logically correct.

When he shouted "Ich hab' hunger" (I am hungry), I tried to re-inforce his use of speech by immediately feeding him tea by mouth, rather than through the nasogastric tube. (Solid food through the mouth was out of the question—he might have breathed it into his lungs.) The doctors feared that he might not swallow the tea, but he did. Here was progress indeed!

Moshe now began to speak more frequently in reaction to other people's speech. When a friend brought him regards from a colleague, he thanked him in German. Likewise, when asked his name, he gave the correct answer. When I asked him to repeat something I had not heard clearly, he said: "Ich hab' keine Absicht" (I have no such inten-tion). Asked to give his age, he answered "Ich weiss nicht" (I don't know) and the next day "Eighty-five." At least he answered with a number.

Moshe now said Hebrew words occasionally—words like kindle and fast-day. And he reacted to Hebrew prayers. When I intoned "Our Father, our King," in Hebrew from the Rosh Hashanah service, he completed one of the lines of the prayer correctly. He said the She'ma prayer with Alon, who would say the first two words of each sentence while Moshe completed it. We soon found that Moshe remembered the entire first and third verses of the *She'ma*, and he would recite them.

Moshe frequently reacted in German when someone spoke English. To my "You are in hospital," he replied, "Ich bin zu Hause" (I am at home). From time to time he would also translate certain words or phrases from one language to another, for instance, from German into English, when he said: "Seite, page" or from Hebrew into German: "ta'azov, lass sein" (leave it). I could not fathom why he did this. It was certainly not to make himself better understood since he was speaking to me, and I know all three languages. Occasionally he translated a phrase like "leave me" into Hebrew, for the nurses' benefit.

Moshe now began to nod and shake his head appropriately as a form of nonverbal communication. I recalled how, with Rodney's encouragement, we had unsuccessfully tried to achieve this objective several weeks earlier.

Numbers continued to fascinate Moshe, but now they were often incorporated into German sentences, as in: "Ich hab' gesagt 340, 360" (I said 340, 360). He seemed particularly interested in ages, even if they were not realistic: "Ich bin in den neunziger Jahren" (I am in my nineties) or: "Sie hat gesagt sie ist 440" (She said she is 440).

Moshe could be quite emphatic in his use of language. When I asked him whether certain friends had come to see him, he replied, "Ich weiss nichts" (I know nothing). On another occasion he said, "Ich will nichts" (I want nothing).

Thirteen weeks after his operation he started to swear vociferously. First there were expressions like "damn it" in English and "Verfluchte, Verdreckte" (cursed, filthy one) in German. Moshe also had recourse to blasphemous curses like "Jesus Maria." Additional signs of aggression also appeared: Moshe constantly tried to silence us with "ruhig" (quiet) or "shh." This silencing was accompanied by his hitting the person near him with his hand or elbow.

At this time he reacted more frequently to what people said, although still exclusively in German. When I told him that Alon and Yona had been to see him, his response was: "Vielleicht" (perhaps).

He had a standard answer, "Ich weiss nichts" (I know nothing), for many of my questions, such as "What is my name?" or "Did Jonathan tell you he wants to get married?" But when I asked him whether he wanted his legs covered, he replied, "Will nicht bedeckt haben" (don't want to be covered).

On Yom Kippur eve, Moshe suddenly began to perspire profusely and to roll his eyes uncontrollably. A series of tests revealed that he had hypoglycemia (low blood sugar) related to the medication he was taking for his diabetes. Upon returning to the ward after the tests, he was extremely angry and screamed "Mord" (murder) and "Scheisse" (shit). This seemed clearly to be a reaction to the tests to which he had been subjected. A nurse approached him to take a blood sample and he said in Hebrew "Enough" and "Leave me." I tried to persuade him to let the nurse take the blood sample, saying, "We have to do that." He answered, "We don't have to do anything." He cursed in English but responded to Bayla's Yom Kippur wishes politely in Hebrew: "Thank you."

Jonathan visited Moshe later that day and was rewarded by the greatest gift of all: Moshe's calling him by his term of endearment, "Plussy," and adding, "You are my son." At last Jonathan had absolute proof that Moshe recognized him.

When the nurse asked Moshe in Hebrew if he was feeling well, he answered "Yes." When she inquired whether he had pain he replied: "No." She continued her questions: "How old are you?" His response, "Sixty," was the first time he had stated his age correctly, probably due to guess-work.

But asked "What is your profession?" he responded, "Tailor."

"Where are you from?"

"China."

These answers had nothing to do with Moshe's reality, and we had no idea why he gave them. I do not believe he was able to pull anyone's leg as yet.

The high point of the day was when Moshe said to Jonathan: "Ich will lesen" (I want to read). Jonathan wrote a special text on a card for him in large capital letters. The message was "ICH LIEBE DICH" (I love you). Moshe studied the card for a while, moving his lips. Jonathan begged him to read the text aloud and Moshe finally did so. Both Jonathan and the relatives of the other patients in Moshe's room were overjoyed. Moshe could actually read! Here was yet another complicated achievement, dependent on high cognitive functioning, which had come out of the deep freeze.

I prepared German reading-cards with messages about where Moshe was and why, the fact that we missed him at home, and that he was improving daily. But Moshe absolutely refused to look at these cards during the next few weeks. Nor did he take kindly to similar cards in English and Hebrew. In fact, they all provoked his anger.

But that day, when Moshe read "ICH LIEBE DICH," Jonathan felt he was alert enough now to understand his great news and told him about his plans to marry Yona. Moshe reacted in English: "If she wants." This gave Jonathan the green light to announce his engagement.

Thinking over those eventful hours, the thought crossed my mind that Moshe's tremendous progress might have been due to his hypoglycemia earlier that day. Was it possible, perhaps, that this pathological condition had affected Moshe's brain positively? With great hesitation I decided to present my theory to one of the physicians.

"Even if your hunch were correct, we could not do anything about it," he said, adding, "One cannot afford to play around with the blood sugar—it could lead to death."

The following day, Yom Kippur, Moshe's aggression reappeared. I had decided to spend most of the day with him, as I had done ten days earlier during Rosh Hashanah, when I read the prayers aloud. For both days of Rosh Hashanah, our friend Harold had come to the hospital to blow the *Shofar* (ram's horn) for Moshe, who had totally ignored it.

I had planned to read aloud the most important Yom Kippur prayers. Moshe objected at once: "Ich will nichts von Juden hören" (I don't want to hear anything to do with Jews). To my question whether he was a Jew, he replied "Quatsch" (rubbish). "Ärgerlich" (angry) and "Gemeinheiten" (nastiness) followed. When I started the famous prayer "Our Father, our King," he shouted "Nein, Scheisse" (No, shit). "We are guilty," I began the litany of sins; Moshe countered it with a swear word. "We have betrayed thee," I continued. He reacted with another curse. I realized there was no point in my continuing to recite these prayers, since I was only upsetting him.

Following Yom Kippur, Moshe said very little for a couple of days, and I had to be reminded that development never proceeds without plateaus.

❖ ❖ ❖ 15 ❖ ❖ ❖

# Negativism

Much of Moshe's speech consisted of curses, negative statements, and accusations.

"Not me" was his response when I told him that we all loved him; "No, no, you don't do anything" when I pointed out that I was trying to help him; and "I don't believe it" when I assured him that he was improving. Hearing that everyone was waiting for him to get well, he responded "gelogen" (it's a lie). I repeated to him, often, that I too was very angry about his illness and prolonged stay in the hospital, but he declared that this was not so.

It was fourteen weeks after his bypass, and Moshe was negative to one and all. Thus, when Jonathan again wrote him a card with "WE LOVE YOU" on it, Moshe called him "verfluchtes Tier" (cursed animal). He averted his gaze from Shirley, Bill, and me when we visited him. To my request that he look at us, he replied, "Ich will nicht" (I don't want to). No, he didn't want to drink, he said when asked, adding "Shit." Shirley told him that I had reported his great progress to her.

Moshe's response: "Esther doesn't tell the truth."

Shirley persisted: "Many people say you're making progress."

"No they don't."

The negativity continued during the following weeks. The family got the brunt of it. Once when I stroked him, Moshe said, "Nobody wants to be stroked. Terrible you. Damn you as a wife." He even hit the baby, although he had earlier smiled at little Elisha and thrown him a ball. On another occasion he said, "I don't want to see you." When I asked if he wanted me to visit him he responded with an emphatic "No." Did he want me to go home? The answer was like-wise "No." He called me "cursed animal," hit me, and told me that he hated me.

I said playfully, "You are hitting a good wife."

"A good wife does not exist."

It was clear that in spite of all his expressions of hatred, Moshe did not want me to leave him. After all, I was the closest person to him —almost an extension of himself—upon whom he could vent all his anger and frustration about his condition.

It seemed as if he had to oppose everything anyone said. Fifteen weeks post-operatively, I said, "Jonathan is a good boy."

Moshe countered, "Don't call him 'good boy.' He's not good."

"Everybody loves him," I insisted.

"No, nobody does."

Moshe contradicted even more neutral statements:

"We can get you a nice book," I promised.

"Nobody wants it, nobody likes it."

As he looked at the passing cars and buses he exclaimed, "No cars, no buses." This meant either that there were no vehicles or that he did not want to see them.

Moshe opposed me even when I agreed with him. For instance, when he said "Accursed time" and I agreed, saying "Certainly," he countered: "Nothing is certain."

Much of Moshe's negativism centered on his illness and the hospi-tal, since he believed "everybody here [at the hospital] is dead" and thought that he would not improve. The continual "no" served as a protest against both his illness and the hospital.

Moshe frequently reminded me of a two-year-old who establishes his or her uniqueness, individuality, and separateness from mother by repeatedly saying "no," thus proving that he or she has a will of his or her own. But the toddler is not wholly negative; he or she also smiles, distributes kisses, and greets you warmly. The toddler's behavior signals yes-and-no, whereas Moshe's speech indicated only no-no, and it was accompanied by a lot of aggression and very few positive expressions of feelings. Yet, as in a small child, Moshe's "no" did not always signal an intention; at times it was merely a declaration of independence. In typical toddler fashion, he said "no" when I asked him whether he wanted some applesauce, but he ate it willingly immediately thereafter (sixteen weeks post-operatively). I sincerely hoped that the negativism would be a passing phenomenon, as it is in the toddler.

Moshe had been verbally aggressive before his illness—he said the most outrageous things to near and dear ones, but always with tongue in cheek. Now he was in deadly earnest. I longed for signs of his old sense of humor. Would it ever reappear? Aggression without the relief of humor seemed frightening and almost inhuman.

From week fifteen Moshe started expressing distress at his condition, in both words and tears. When Rachel, his assistant, told him that Shraga had been sad that Moshe had not spoken to him, he answered in Hebrew, "Tell Shraga that I am miserable" (misken). Five weeks earlier, Dr. Lewis had declared that it would be a medical miracle if Moshe ever spoke again. He now agreed that a miracle had indeed taken place.

Not all of Moshe's speech was linked to anger or sadness. When Rodney introduced himself by name, Moshe reacted appropriately with "From upstairs." But the sad or angry feelings tended to reappear quickly. In response to Rodney's congratulations on Jonathan's engagement, Moshe replied, "What Mazel Tov? Everything is so terrible here."

Rodney frequently assumed the role of educator in Moshe's presence. Once Rodney handed him paper and pen, but Moshe threw it back at him saying: "I don't want to do it" (i.e., write). Rodney reprimanded him: "You are not a child; you are an adult." Earlier, when Moshe spoke to him in German, Rodney told him he did not know that language. Thereupon Moshe grudgingly changed to English, complaining, "English is a stupid language." (By the end of the sixteenth week Moshe was speaking Arabic to the Arab orderlies.) Rodney again stepped into the teacher's role when he told Moshe not to shout at him. Moshe lowered his voice. Usually one could hear Moshe's shouting and cursing all over the corridors.

Rodney, trying to be empathic, said to Moshe, "I know how you feel." Moshe disagreed. "You can't. Nobody knows how I feel. I am dead." For emphasis, he added some swear words like "shit." Rodney, usually a quiet, gentle person, answered, "Shit to you." This stopped Moshe's swearing. He then poured out his heart to Rodney: "It's terrible just sitting all day. I keep saying stupid things." Here were the first signs of insight, which he had mercifully been spared before.

To Jonathan he complained the next day that people made fun of him because of his condition, adding that it was terrible to wake up and not know where you are. Finally: "It's no fun to be in the hospital." That must have been the understatement of the year! Moshe was becoming more aware of his environment. He began to complain about a screaming patient whom he termed "crazy."

Moshe was now starting to define people, objects, and situations with the help of adjectives: "Jonathan is a good boy"; "the patient is crazy"; "Jack is a stupid person"; "I am a miserable soul"; "the juice is bitter and everything is terrible." Before this Moshe's sentences had been composed of nouns, pronouns, and verbs without modifiers.

Moshe was often aphasic, at a loss for the right word. Thus, when he wanted me to write, he said in a circumlocutory way, "Make the signs for the book." He referred to the wheelchair as "the machine" and asked, "Can one do something about this animal thing?" when he meant "this fly."

Frequently he expected me to know what he was unable to express in words. For example, he was very angry one day that I "did not go over there to arrange . . ." When I asked what I was supposed to arrange, he covered up his loss of words by changing reality: "You should know because I have told you often." Unfortunately, this did not help me fulfill his wish. On another occasion he pleaded, "Help me." As if anticipating my unuttered question, he demanded, "Don't ask in what way!" This reminded me of a young child who expects a mother to know what he or she needs without being told.

Moshe also suffered from a particular kind of aphasia in which he would say the opposite of what he meant. He shouted "Get rid of the shoe!" when he wanted me to put his shoe on for him, and he was very angry that I did not understand his intention immediately. He said to Jonathan, "Please leave me," but he obviously meant the opposite because he added, "I don't want to be alone." He screamed "no" when I inquired whether I should bring him a drink, although it was clear that he wanted one badly.

Fortunately, the aphasia soon disappeared.

He also had a fair amount of echolalia (echoing in his speech). To Rodney's compliment, "Elisha is a beautiful grandchild," Moshe replied, "Grandchild." When I asked him, "Do you want to sit down?" he repeated, "Sit down." In answer to a friend's asking, "Are you comfortable?" he echoed, "Comfortable." The echolalia continued for only a few weeks.

Nor was his sentence construction always correct. Thus, sixteen weeks after surgery Moshe cried, "Plussy, where Plussy is?" He frequently called any member of our family "Plussy," which had once been his term of endearment for Jonathan alone.

When Moshe was overly eager to say something he tended to stutter, repeating the first syllable several times. He had never done this before his surgery. The stuttering outlasted all the other speech problems.


❖ ❖ ❖ 16 ❖ ❖ ❖

## Movement

Real progress in motor skills began twelve weeks after Moshe's operation. He now turned himself in bed by holding onto the bedrail and pushing himself away from it. This was a major milestone since it meant he no longer needed two nurses to turn him every two hours. He also no longer needed an air mattress. Shaare Zedek had once tried water mattresses, but all of them had leaked. They now resorted to a foam mattress cut like an egg carton, which prevented sores in a bedridden patient by leaving air spaces.

The most important benefit of this motor skill improvement was that Moshe could turn his back when he did not want to see someone. He used this skill on numerous occasions, finding it even more effective than not looking at the person, which he also resorted to frequently. In the fourteenth week, I showed Moshe a volume of his collected articles and started to read their headings to him. He hit the book and turned away.

In a further motor development, Moshe learned to move his pillow with his right hand to arrange it properly under his head. Here was purposeful action indeed, requiring thought.

Another action that necessitated thought came into force when Moshe took a tissue from Jonathan in order to remove his phlegm and later gestured to him for another tissue. For several weeks Moshe had removed his phlegm with his hands and could not be taught to use a tissue for this purpose. Now we felt more confident about his ability to remember or relearn those habits and manners which we usually take for granted but without which life with people close to us may become irritating and downright unpleasant.

That same week Alon and Moshe played a game. Moshe was supposed to wear a mitten tied on each hand to prevent him from pulling out the nasogastric tube. After taking off the mittens, he and Alon repeatedly threw one of them to each other. This indicated that Moshe was really aware of Alon's presence. Of no less importance was Moshe's ability to engage in an act of reciprocity with a partner.

Soon thereafter (fourteen weeks post-operatively) Yona's parents gave a small party to celebrate her engagement to Jonathan. After the party, Alon and Yossi visited Moshe to tell him about this important event. When Moshe saw Yossi, he pulled up the bedsheet, apparently aware that it was inappropriate to be half nude in the presence of someone who is not close family.

During that same week Moshe took his first few steps, supported by a physiotherapist on each side. Although he moved his feet forward, they had to drag him like a sack of potatoes, since he was unable to support the lower part of his body properly. But he was moving his feet without needing to be reminded to do so. This happened three weeks after Dr. Reisman, chief of geriatrics, had expressed serious doubts that Moshe would ever be able to walk again!

The doctors had also doubted that Moshe would ever be able to relearn everyday procedures like dressing or undressing himself. One of Moshe's first acts to prove them wrong came fifteen weeks after surgery, when he took off his nightshirt, drawing it over his head. He was able to roll the legs of his pajamas up and down and to apply chapstick to his dry lips. He opened a tube of anchovy paste with one hand and spread the paste on his bread with the other. Seventeen weeks after the operation he was able to use a can opener to open a can of tuna.

Going back to week fifteen: when he was seated in his wheelchair, Moshe pushed forward and backward with his feet and used them to brake. He was obviously more in control of his own locomotion now, although far from independent.

❖ ❖ ❖ 17 ❖ ❖ ❖

## Murder

On the threshold of consciousness twelve weeks after his operation, Moshe was furious. He swore continually in German, mostly in my presence. He was especially fond of anal imagery like "asshole" and "shit." Moshe insisted that everything was "stupid," often screaming "Quatsch" (rubbish), with "Blödsinn" (stupidity) thrown in for good measure. "Damn you" became a favorite exclamation in English.

Much of Moshe's verbal aggression was accompanied by physical violence. He would tear off the bandages on his hands with his teeth. The purpose of these bandages was to prevent him from pulling off the condom catheter by means of which he was kept dry. (At Hadassah a catheter had been inserted into his urethra, but prolonged use of this instrument caused repeated urinary infections, accompanied by high temperatures. For this reason they preferred to use the condom catheter at Shaare Zedek.)

What caused me the greatest distress was the fact that Moshe hit me repeatedly.

The following week all this behavior culminated in the grand accusation: "She wants to murder me." He spoke of "a case of murder" and screamed for help. The next day he announced, "I'll murder you," and several days later, while being shaved, he shouted: "Murdered!" He mentioned Sachsenhausen, the concentration camp where his father had been interned for a time in 1938. Later in the week he declared, "I am murdered" and "I hate you" and screamed intermittently.

In the fifteenth week, Moshe expressed similar attitudes and beliefs to Yona's father. When Yossi said to him, "Moshe, look at me," Moshe answered, "I don't want to. You doctors killed me." Yossi argued with him: "But you are not dead." "I am," Moshe persisted.

He became more upset in the sixteenth week. With tears in his eyes, he cried, "I am dead. You are dead. I am murdered," and accused, "You have done nothing for me. You have no love for me. Bloody wife, nothing good for me. I don't want to see you. I want to get rid of you. I want to have her murdered." I felt true pity for him in his torment. It was terrible that none of my protestations carried any power of conviction for him.

He was now more aware of his environment, in which he saw many old people sitting there just staring ahead of them. Moshe interpreted it differently: "Everybody here is dead."

Not only did his standard repertoire of curses remain in force but his physical violence increased. He twisted my hand, tried to kick me, and frequently hit me with his hand, fist, or elbow. I was careful to sit at his left side, which was considerably weaker than his right, so that the blows would be less painful. On one occasion he brought my hand up to his mouth as if to bite it, but dropped it at the last moment.

Throughout this time I saw Moshe as a patient rather than as a husband. This prevented me from feeling anything personal in his attacks. I tried to understand him and to empathize with him, thus minimizing feelings of hurt or insult. Besides, his aggression was a sign that he was regaining consciousness, and I considered that whatever price I would have to pay for that would not be too high. But I did occasionally try to cajole him out of his aggression. When he hit me with his elbow, I playfully did the same to him, only to be told, "It is ridiculous to attack me." When he shouted at me, I shouted back at him mockingly.

Very gradually I started allowing myself to feel those emotions that

I had tried to hold at bay during the past dreadful months, so as to be able to carry on with daily living. I realized that I could no longer play hide-and-seek with my fears and apprehensions, faced as I was with Moshe in his present state. There was no doubt that he had come a long, long way since the days when he could not even open his eyes. But in whose presence did I find myself now?

I hardly dared admit it to myself. Here was a man who combined the features of a helpless, miserable patient with those of a rude, unmannerly child and a demanding tyrant, without concern for anyone but himself. I was equally perturbed about Moshe's mental state, which was highly confused—many of his statements sounded quite crazy. All in all, a far cry from the man I had loved and married! Oh Lord, what kind of person had I helped bring back to life? Was this the man for whose recovery I had so fervently prayed?

Where was my quick-witted, humorous, sensitive, insightful husband, who had always been ready to help those who came to him for advice? He had been no paragon of virtue. On occasion he flew off the handle and then refused to admit that he had been at fault. But through these reminiscences about his merits and imperfections, I reconstructed Moshe in my mind as a whole human being, as the man to whom I had become attracted and attached. Would he ever again have a multifaceted personality?

As I looked at him in the hospital ward I felt more than a little guilty for allowing myself to harbor so much resentment toward a man who had undergone such a terrifying trauma, one from which he seemed to be slowly recovering at long last. Why should I resign myself now to sharing the future with a sad, bad, mad Moshe when he was improving noticeably from day to day?

Watching his progress, I became more hopeful about the outcome of his condition, until I finally gained the upper hand over my fears. With the support of my children—so I believed—I would steer Moshe toward becoming the kind of person he had formerly been. What a challenge! If only we could be steadfast enough to sustain him on the long and arduous journey.

The neurologists and psychiatrists spoke of a "disinhibition syndrome," characterized by the lack of all normal rules of social conduct and lack of concern for the consequences of one's actions. They attributed this syndrome to injury of the frontal lobes of the brain. But was there not another way to understand Moshe's fury and violence?*

It seemed to me that, having become more conscious and more aware of his miserable physical and mental state, Moshe had constructed the following explanation to account for his condition. I, as his wife and therefore the one closest to him, must be responsible for what had happened to him. So I had intended to murder him or had actually done so. What could he do in return but wish to murder me? After all, as we were to learn, Moshe had absolutely no recollection then or later of the illness preceding his operation, of the operation itself, or of his subsequent coma. Here was a person who had entered the hospital able to move all parts of his body at will and in full control of his mental faculties. Now, thirteen weeks post-operatively, he was totally helpless and dependent on other people to carry out all his most basic needs: although he could just about turn himself in bed, he could not eat and had no sphincter control. To explain his painful predicament, Moshe needed to generate a theory that made sense of the imperfect and incomplete data then available to him.

To outsiders it must have seemed as if Moshe were fighting a long-standing battle with me. They probably supposed that the true nature of our relationship was now coming into the open. Fortunately, I felt reasonably confident that our marital relationship prior to the surgery had been good. Therefore I had no need to defend myself to anyone and did not feel too embarrassed or humiliated by Moshe's public expressions of anger toward me. We had usually expressed anger at appropriate times and had on the whole managed to resolve conflicts as they arose. I did not feel that Moshe's present anger was due to an accumulation of resentment or hostility that he had not previously been able to express.

One of the geriatricians of the unit commiserated with me but regretted he could not help. He did not know whether Moshe's aggression would be a transitory or permanent phenomenon. I kept up

*I could not judge how much of Moshe's asocial, violent behavior was an inevitable consequence of frontal-lobe damage and how much might have been determined by Moshe's disposition. He seemed to be reacting in anger to frustrations and impotence and to the physical state and environment in which he found himself.

my optimism by talking to relatives of patients who had had strokes or had suffered some other form of brain damage. They assured me that their loved ones had gone through a similar angry phase that ultimately passed. So I told myself that it was only a matter of time before Moshe abandoned this behavior.

Dr. Frisch, the psychiatrist who saw Moshe at this stage, found him completely uncommunicative but also experienced the brunt of his anger and lack of inhibition. A week later, after we had reported that Moshe was speaking in complicated sentences, Dr. Frisch saw him again. But again he could not "get in touch" with Moshe. In fact, Moshe turned his back on him and at the most nodded or shook his head. He touched his genitals while being addressed and made bird-like noises or closed his eyes when he was supposed to listen, as if to block the doctor out of his awareness.

At about this time, Dr. Gold, a cardiologist friend of my brother Gershon from Los Angeles, came to visit Moshe. He told me he would never be able to face Gershon again if he did not give him an eye-witness report about Moshe. He met Moshe sitting in the corridor of the chronic geriatric unit, tied to his wheelchair. Although he tried to engage him in conversation, Moshe replied only by shouting "Quatsch" (rubbish) repeatedly.

Dr. Gold called my brother only a month later. "I have nothing good to report," he said to Gershon. "I don't think your brother-in-law will ever regain full consciousness."

"I have news for you," my brother replied. "He has already done so."

❖

Moshe was a greatly changed man. He had lost one third of his former weight and was now underweight at 60 kilos (132 pounds). A friend later told me he thought Moshe looked like someone in the terminal stage of cancer. His hair was very thin and gray, and there were large bald patches on the back of his head, from bedsores. Oddly enough, these bald patches upset me more than anything else about Moshe's outward appearance. For me they symbolized the dreadful state to which he had been reduced.

I used to wheel Moshe to a quiet corner in the waiting room of the children's nephrology department to obtain a semblance of privacy.

But after a few days the staff there asked me to take him somewhere else since both his appearance and his shouting and cursing were likely to frighten the children.

❖ ❖ ❖ 18 ❖ ❖ ❖

## "Useless You, Helpless I"

Fifteen weeks after his heart surgery, Moshe seemed conscious, but very angry and confused. We knew that he had made a giant leap forward, out of a semi-conscious condition; he now spoke more frequently in response to what went on around him and usually—but not always—within a given context. Moreover, Moshe was now able to react appropriately to requests and commands, so that when Jonathan asked him to say "Please" and "Thank you" he did so. He pulled up his pants on request, said "God bless you" when I told him to do so after I sneezed, and lowered his voice when Rodney asked him not to shout. He did not always cooperate, but at least we knew that he was able to do so.

So Moshe had finally emerged out of his coma, slowly and almost imperceptibly, not with a bang but with a whimper. It was a seamless transition. We hardly realized that the great event for which we had so eagerly hoped and prayed had appeared at long last, unaccompanied by thunder and lightning.

For us Moshe's reawakening is associated with the reemergence of his humor. It was crude at first, but who cared? On October 12, fifteen weeks after his operation, Moshe said to Alon as he watched me walking away from him, "Mummy waves her *tochis* [ass]." Seeing Alon laugh at his remark, he cried and laughed at the same time, and exclaimed, "Lonny is laughing, funny." He also laughed when Alon reported that Yossi had promised to eat his hat if Moshe ever became fully conscious. I was delighted that Moshe had regained his ability to laugh, although his laughter at first was often mingled with tears. He realized three weeks later that he cried whenever he became excited.

It was far from easy sailing, even now. Sixteen weeks after surgery, Moshe began to show insight into his state, and his mental suffering increased. "How terrible it is to be in this condition!" he complained. "I have no *sechel* [intelligence], I keep saying stupid things." He asked, "Don't you know what an idiot I am?" He received a psychiatrist friend, crying, "Janshi, look at someone who has died. Can you explain this?" Janshi gave him a factual explanation of recent events, while Alon quoted Proverbs 3.12: "Whom the Lord loves He rebukes." Whereupon Moshe exclaimed, "Your theology!" Hardly lacking in intelligence, as we told him.

Moshe asked me point-blank, "How come you made your husband suffer?" I assured him that this was the last thing I wanted to happen —his suffering was a consequence of his heart surgery. He claimed to know this but added, "I am killed."

He termed the nurses' assurances that he had greatly improved "a false belief." Two weeks later (eighteen weeks after the surgery), somebody pointed out to him that he was much better than he had been the previous week. He called this "making fun of me." On being told that the doctors were happy with his improvement, he declared, "They don't know anything."

Moshe seemed altogether baffled about his physical and mental state. He pointed to the large scar on his right leg, as if to ask how it had gotten there. I explained that a vein had been removed from this leg for the coronary bypass. He listened and even suggested that I write it down—he had already become aware that I was taking notes about him, which I had started when he was still in Hadassah Hospital.

Moshe's considerable confusion at times caused me unnecessary inconvenience. For example, sitting in his wheelchair in the plaza of the hospital, Moshe expressed a need to go to the toilet. I wheeled him back to the elevator and took him upstairs. Once in his ward, he became angry that I should have thought he wanted to use the toilet.

Amid this welter of confusion and misery Moshe needed some means of comforting himself. He therefore frequently played with himself, apparently quite unconcerned about the presence of others.

In this he resembled a young child who does not realize that touching the genitalia is considered a private activity.

Moshe continued to be extremely impatient and self-centered. If we had to wait for the elevator to arrive, he shouted "Move!" Once the elevator was completely full. He commanded, "Damn, take her out. Some people are not entitled to the elevator. They are idiots."

His negativism was still directed primarily at me. When I told him he would get well and teach again, he shouted in German, "No, shit, shit, shit!" Once he denied that we were married and declared that he wanted no family.

One day Moshe called me "Crazy woman, because you understand everything wrongly, you don't know what you are talking about." Was he projecting his bewilderment onto me? Worse was still to come. "You haven't proved yourself," he accused. "Nobody helps me. You are nobody. Useless you, helpless I. I hate you." So this is how it looked from his point of view. He was entirely right, of course: I had been useless when he was so helpless. But was he really in a position to judge me? I was sober-minded enough to realize that I had stood by him throughout his terrible illness and had tried my utmost on his behalf. I knew that if I had failed it was not for lack of good intentions or for want of trying. Yet I could not convey any of this to him in his present condition. I could but hope that he would understand one day.

Moshe now did not want to receive any visitors and instructed me not to let anyone in. When I mentioned to him that Elisha was about to be brought in, he said that he did not want any baby, "damn it." Yet once he saw the little fellow Moshe cried and called out "Schnubbel," his term of love. To my mother, who had just arrived from London, he said, "I don't want to see you. Turn around." The only time she got an affirmative answer out of him was when she asked if she should go home. Later, I asked if there was anyone he wanted to see, and he answered, "no."

"Alon?" I specified.

"Is different."

"Jonathan?"

"Is different."

So it appeared that Moshe was able to differentiate between his immediate family and those more distant from him. He did not want me to go home at all. "You are not supposed to leave," he said. "You don't go."

Moshe did not want to know about mail we had received. I mentioned that I had had a letter from Gershon. "I don't want to hear from him," Moshe said. I told him about a letter from two of his cousins and he replied, "Two unwelcome people." When I reported the numerous phone calls I had received, he responded, "Get rid of calls. No good. Let them go to hell. It doesn't interest me." I asked whether he was interested only in his recovery and he replied, "Nothing else."

Moshe also wanted nothing to do with the radio, books, or television. I asked the nurse to let him see the news on television but he would have none of it, explaining to her in Hebrew, "I have enough troubles of my own." Who could blame him for this attitude? The nurse argued, "But your wife requests it." His answer was right on the ball: "My wife requests a lot of things, but I don't always want them."

❖ ❖ ❖ 19 ❖ ❖ ❖

Food

Once he was out of his coma we tried to get Moshe to eat by mouth. During the previous few weeks he had repeatedly pulled out his nasogastric tube in spite of having his hands bandaged or restrained with mittens. It was torture every time the nurses forced the tube in again. But without his gag reflex, the tube was necessary to prevent him from breathing food into his lungs.

At Hadassah Moshe had been given a highly concentrated canned liquid diet, containing all the necessary nutrients, which slowly dripped into his stomach via the tube. At Shaare Zedek the nurses had put pureed meat and vegetable soups or liquified fruit or milk products into a syringe whose contents they discharged into Moshe's stomach via the tube. We smiled at Moshe's tolerance for milk products when administered in this way, because he had always claimed that he was allergic to them from his infancy. Now it became apparent that the allergy was not physical.

It was clear to the staff as well as to us that Moshe would have to use his mouth to eat again now that he was conscious. After the doctor had established that Moshe was able to swallow liquified food, we tried to spoonfeed him. But he refused, declaring, "Ich will nicht essen" (I don't want to eat). I reminded him that he had always loved to eat. In fact he used to eat far more than was good for his health. That this same man now refused food was a real irony.

I tried to cajole him into eating.

"Perhaps you would like an egg?"

"I don't want anything from you. I want to get rid of you," was the response.

The administrator of the unit, Mrs. Nathan, tried to feed Moshe herself, but he protested, "I don't want anything." A little earlier, though, he had told her for the first time that he wanted to go home. That was a wish we all seconded eagerly.

One of the nurses finally managed to feed him an egg. But this was not enough food to sustain him; he still had to get most of his nourishment via the nasogastric tube. He fought having the tube reinserted. I began to fear that Moshe might slowly starve to death.

Eventually one of the doctors managed the feat of reinserting the tube. Moshe drank some Coke but refused grapefruit juice, complaining that it was bitter, which was quite true. "Everything is terrible," he cried. The next day we were delighted to see him drink from a cup and even put the empty cup on a chair next to him. Also he ate half an apple and half a banana, which he peeled himself. Another major step occurred when he put a spoonful of mashed fruit into his mouth. This was a good start but no more than a start. Moshe was still not eating sufficiently on his own to relinquish the tube.

Mrs. Nathan now invested much of her pride and energy in getting Moshe to eat. Aware of Moshe's anger toward me, she wisely decided not to let me attempt to feed him. Instead she assigned him a sweet young German orderly. The girl sat next to Moshe's bed for a long time and patiently did her utmost to persuade him to eat some apple puree, but to no avail. Mrs. Nathan did not give up, however.

At the next mealtime, she gave Moshe a choice of foods. Again the reaction was negative. Thereupon she asked him if he wanted to go on a hunger strike. "Don't make fun of me," Moshe reproved her.

On a visit that week, Beyla and I wheeled Moshe down to the cafeteria. We offered to buy him any food he wanted. Unfortunately the choice was neither large nor tempting—primarily sandwiches and chocolate bars. Moshe wanted only a Coke. He refused to touch the egg sandwich I brought him.

But two weeks after waking up fully (seventeen weeks after his operation), Moshe ate breakfast in the presence of Shraga, his assistant, who made it his business to be there at breakfast as often as possible. For lunch Moshe had a three-course meal, including meat.

He was now eating with such gusto that when a volunteer came at lunchtime to ask if Moshe wanted help in putting on his phylacteries, Moshe gave his consent but continued to eat while saying his prayers.

A few days later, when the nurse asked him whether he wanted an omelette, Moshe nodded but said he was afraid that the toast would be with cheese. He ate what he had ordered, praising it ("Good food") and the staff ("Decent people"). I asked him if he wanted something to drink. "Damn you, to say bad things," he growled. Clearly, his ambivalence toward food reflected his feelings toward the person who was associated with eating. It was similar to a young child who has eating problems in the presence of the mother with whom he is in conflict. However, soon thereafter Moshe started eating in my presence also.

Once he said to us as he was eating, "The food is half past decent" (instead of "halfway decent"). We teased him about that and he joined in the laughter.

Alon brought Moshe ice cream and he asked for more. He also ate fish that Yona brought him from home. On one of Yossi's frequent visits, Moshe complained of feeling hungry and asked for something to eat. Yossi, eager to fulfill Moshe's wish, searched for edibles in Moshe's night-table. Finally he found a box of cookies, only to be reprimanded by Mrs. Nathan, who reminded him, the physician, that Moshe, a diabetic, must on no account be given any food containing sugar. Clearly Mrs. Nathan was unaware of the ice cream he had eaten.

Moshe was now consuming the hospital meals, which were prepared according to each patient's special needs and wishes. I was happy to hear him praise the food: "Best food—better than at home," getting in a dig at me. "It's too good," he said to the dietician. Yet he frequently complained that the hospital food was too spicy.

I suggested to the dietician that Moshe should have more calcium in his food. When the dietician asked him if he wanted food with calcium, Moshe got a shock, believing calcium to be the name of an illness. He asked who had invented that illness—"yet another one!" Poor Moshe, he really felt we were making him suffer.

❖ ❖ ❖ 20 ❖ ❖ ❖

# Rehabilitation

From the time he regained full consciousness fifteen weeks after surgery, Moshe needed to be resocialized, starting with the necessary body cleanliness. When I suggested that he should have his nails cleaned, he asked, "Why do we have to get clean?" Asked whether he wanted a toothbrush, he accused me of having "terrible ideas." Yet he brushed his teeth properly the next day and every following day. With the orderly who tried to shave him, he pleaded in Hebrew, "I am scared, do me a favor." So I shaved him myself with his own electric shaver until he protested even about that. But two weeks after regaining full consciousness he asked to be shaved.

At about the same time I asked whether I could comb his hair. He reacted angrily: "I don't want you to do anything for me. It is offensive to me." Moshe had always been an independent person and was obviously returning to the old pattern, where he wanted to do everything himself. Five weeks out of coma, when I told him to use a tissue to cough into, he merely said, "My inspector."

We had worried about how to go about Moshe's toilet training. Even more worrying was the question whether he would lose sphincter control permanently due to neurological damage. But less than a week elapsed from the time he regained consciousness until he was clean and dry, except when he had to wait to be taken to the toilet because the nurses and orderlies were occupied. He called wetting himself "this impossible situation." A day or two after his "return," he told Yona how terrible it had been for him to soil himself. When Jonathan told me to remind Moshe to use the toilet, Moshe became upset and demanded, "Stop giving me instructions." In reaction to my question whether he needed the bottle for passing urine in bed, he expressed his emphatic refusal almost poetically: "*Will ich nicht, soll ich nicht, brauch' ich nicht*" (I want not, I must not, I need not).

On the first Sabbath after he regained consciousness, Moshe was reconnected to the condom catheter since there were not enough nurses or orderlies to attend to him when he needed to be taken to the toilet. I spoke to Mrs. Nathan about the difficulty of training a patient to be dry if the staff was not consistent about it. She agreed with me and gave the appropriate instructions the following Sabbath.

Two weeks after waking up, Moshe became very angry when I praised him for using the toilet appropriately. "Why does one have to talk about it? Grown-up people don't talk about it." How right he was! I had believed that I had to treat him like a little child who has to be praised for using the toilet. I should have related to Moshe as an adult.

A few days later, Moshe asked me to accompany him to the toilet and to stay with him there, since I was his wife. He cleaned himself, and while I went out to get an orderly to help him up from the toilet-seat, he managed to stand up unaided. Finally, he asked to wash his hands. Moshe was becoming more independent each day and remembering old habits connected with personal cleanliness.

Three weeks after fully recovering consciousness, he reported a bad dream in which he had soiled himself. It turned out that he had in fact done so, and he was very upset about it.

A week thereafter his sense of social propriety had fully returned. "I don't like the girls [orderlies] coming in the morning and exposing me," he complained. They undressed him in order to wash him, and there were no curtains around the beds in that unit.

Around this time Alon summarized Moshe's recent accomplishments for him. He had written a letter, put on his phylacteries and taken them off, brushed his teeth, read a German text and translated it instantly into English, gotten up from his wheelchair and walked to the toilet unaided in order to urinate. Moshe's response to this long list was: "Pee-pee is the main thing." Clearly, he felt that his independence around the toilet crowned all his other achievements. Not only did it make him feel fully adult again but, more important, it spared him the humiliation of being unable to control his bodily functions.

Less than a week after he awoke fully, he remembered or quickly relearned socially expected phrases, saying "Thank you" without being prodded when he was given the glass of water he had requested. Only a few days earlier, when I had thanked Jonathan in his presence for helping to put Moshe's shoes on, Moshe said, "Why does one have to use your shit word?"

Two weeks after regaining consciousness (seventeen weeks postoperatively), Moshe used his knife and fork correctly without any coaching from me. His table manners were as good as they had previously been.

Professionals helped Moshe with much of his physical rehabilitation, starting about a week *before* he regained full consciousness. He willingly cooperated with Shoshana, the occupational therapist, telling her, "I want to work with you. You are good. Let's see if this works." He made a fist, opened his hand, and threw beanbags as instructed. After a short while he protested in German, "I don't want to continue." Yet he scribbled on the line when she supplied him with pen and paper.

I usually wheeled him to his physiotherapy sessions. Moshe followed the requests of the physiotherapist, Adina, a lovely young woman from the United States. He stood up when she asked him to do so, saying, "Her wish is my command." But he complained about the exercises she had him do, calling them "terrible." He cried when he thought he could not do something and exclaimed, "I am terrible." Two weeks later, he was afraid that Adina had broken his foot. "These ladies are killers," he said about all the physiotherapists. He insisted that Adina was destroying him, that she had a destructive character, and that she was wicked. She took his admonishments in good spirits, never personally, and remained calm and gentle as always.

Moshe referred to his physiotherapy as "half-days of punishment." Adina took it in good spirits. When she wondered if he remembered her name, Moshe replied, "Last time it was Adina." He was angry when I sang her praises to him and theorized, "She's your girl. You are terribly infatuated with her. A love affair."

He disliked Adina's imposing her will on him. Moshe also resented the games he had to play in physiotherapy, such as throwing rings. "That an old Jew like me should have to play such games!" he complained. "I have only one bottom, which has been broken five times in these so-called games!" The way he saw it was, "I get the *tsures* [troubles] while she gets the *naches* [satisfaction]."

It delighted us that Moshe was able to cooperate and that he knew what he liked and disliked and could express this so clearly. He was no longer a passive, suffering individual for whom others had to do things. He was now able to determine the acts of others in relation to himself to a significant extent. His physical progress was truly amazing: only one day out of coma, during a home visit, he walked up the stairs to our apartment, supported on each side. And two weeks after that he was walking independently, holding only a walker with both hands. At around that time, the nurse once found him sitting on the floor next to his bed. He had wanted to investigate the reason for the noise outside his room and had therefore got out of his bed—over the handrail—on his own. Obviously he needed a higher bedrail for his own safety. Since such bedrails are not available in Israel, we had to convince him that he might seriously hurt himself if he continued to climb out of bed before he was really ready for it. After all, the last thing on earth he needed was to fracture a limb.

Three weeks out of his coma, Moshe almost managed to stand up without help. He no longer needed anyone to accompany him as he went with his walker along the corridor to the doctor's room. There he saw my mother and uncle one day and cried as he waved to them.

# ❖ ❖ ❖ 21 ❖ ❖ ❖
## Home Visit

It was Alon's suggestion, a few days before Moshe regained full consciousness, that he be allowed to come home for a visit. The idea was mind-boggling to me at first. Was Moshe really ready for this, and how would we cope with the technical problems involved? Alon insisted that it was important for Moshe's improvement that he get a taste of home. His certainty once again put my doubts at rest.

Mrs. Nathan was delighted at the idea of the home visit. With her assistance we arranged for a male orderly to accompany Moshe to our home.

October 13, one day after he awakened, was Moshe's first visiting day. It was a glorious day, full of sunshine and warmth, as if the sun itself was happy at the turn of events. As Alon wheeled Moshe toward our car, I could not stop the flow of my tears. This was a day I had never dared picture even to myself during Moshe's coma. Yet now it had come to pass—just nine days short of four months since Moshe's coronary bypass.

Moshe had no recollection of our car or of the name of the street on which we had lived for twenty-three years. But when we arrived at our house, he walked a few steps to the wheelchair, supported on one side by Alon and by Lazer, the orderly, on the other. He was supported up the five steps to our apartment. We were amazed to see that he walked up these steps with alternate feet, unlike a young child starting to climb stairs.

Awaiting him at home were Tamara and the baby. The baby was the first person Moshe noticed, and when Alon called out: "Elisha," Moshe exclaimed, "Little Schnubbel."

At home Moshe spoke only in English, as he had always done in the past. He looked around and exclaimed, "Aren't we lucky?" after which he complimented Lazer: "You did a great job." He excused his rather poor walking with "I can't do better." We asked if he remembered the living room. He claimed that he did. But he did not remember in which direction he had to turn to reach the bathroom.

Later, reading A. R. Luria's book *The Man with a Shattered World* (1987 p. 53), I came across the description of a patient who had sustained a gunshot wound to the head in Russia during World War II. One of his innumerable problems was that he kept losing his way at home: "When I came out of the bathroom, I forgot which way I had to turn to get back to my room. I tried to figure out where my room was, looked around everywhere, but couldn't get the layout of things and decide which way to go."

Moshe addressed both our sons by their names and asked how old Elisha was. Unasked, he volunteered, "I feel better." But his swearing did return when he reproached me: "Damn you, you are constantly making suggestions." We laughed at that and he joined us in our laughter. He also cried easily.

I reminded Moshe that he had been examined by a rehabilitation specialist from Los Angeles who had told us that he was improving. "How does anybody know?" Moshe wondered.

Alon said, "Others like you have improved."

"Don't lecture me," Moshe countered. We felt that the old Moshe was reasserting himself.

At lunch, Moshe sat in his usual place, which had remained empty throughout his long illness. It was really like old times, except that Moshe ate hardly anything. After a while he even became abusive about it: "Damn you for food."

After Moshe had had his afternoon nap in his own bed, Alon decided to show him home movies of the family taken at a time when he and Jonathan were small. Moshe recognized the boys and cried as he identified them, calling them by their terms of endearment. As I explained a certain movie to him, he snapped, "Stop talking nonsense as usual." He was sure that he knew better than I what was being shown and corrected me (wrongly) about the country in which the scene had taken place.

During the showing of these short films Moshe exclaimed, "I haven't yet been able to die!" Later, I told him that Dr. Benson, his surgeon, would visit him. He reacted, "I don't know him. You are the one who knows him." That statement was absolutely correct. Moshe was suffering from retrograde amnesia and had no recollection of the events preceding his operation, such as his first meeting with Dr. Benson, or of the events during the coma.

He reproved me for nothing in particular: "Be a bit understanding! For days I have been trying to get through to you."

We had all been a little apprehensive about whether Moshe would agree to return to the hospital in the evening. To make the transition as easy as possible, Alon had decided he would stay at the hospital as long as was necessary for Moshe to settle back in again. We were relieved that Moshe put up no resistance when we told him the staff were expecting him in the ward. He got a great welcome from the nurses on his return.

The second home visit took place three days later. As Moshe got out of the car, Tamar, a neighbor, greeted him warmly. Moshe responded with the royal plural: "We are too busy to talk!" He had to concentrate so hard on walking that he had no energy left for socializing.

When Moshe saw Elisha he said in German, "The little man is better than all the others." He greeted my uncle: "How are you, Werner?" and addressed my mother as "Oma" (grandmother), as he had been accustomed to do.

We ate breakfast and lunch together—we still had to feed him to some extent. I had prepared his favorite dishes, which he both enjoyed and praised. He was aware of everyone at the table and even worried that Uncle Werner had no food on his plate. Here was clear evidence that Moshe was beginning to be concerned again about other people.

While we were all sitting at the table, Moshe complained that he had not realized it was Rosh Chodesh, the beginning of a new Jewish month, when the doctor had asked him the date that morning. Nor had he known what time it was. He considered his ignorance humiliating. Moshe rightly felt indignant that the doctor had tested him without first giving him a chance to orient himself about the date.

When Moshe became fully conscious, I had brought him a watch with clear numerals in order to help him keep track of time. The words King Ahasuerus had said to his Queen Esther had reverberated in my head: "Whatever your request, even to the half of the kingdom, it shall be given to you." This time the roles were reversed: Esther wanted to satisfy her king and tried to supply his needs before he even became aware of them. Unfortunately, the watch, together with a pen and a radio, had been stolen.

After lunch Moshe asked to use the toilet. In order to save him the walk to the bathroom, Lazer offered him the condom catheter. Moshe's reaction was vehement: "God forbid." He wanted to be left alone on the toilet and insisted that we close the door. We were barely able to prevent him from locking it. He was beginning to regain modesty less than a week after regaining full consciousness.

Again and again Moshe amazed us that day. Dr. Rachmilevitch, one of the grand old men of Israeli medicine, had died that week. Alon wondered aloud what his specialty had been. "Internal medicine," Moshe shot back. Obviously his long-term memory was coming out of the deep freeze. He also recalled that our friend Zvi had visited him in the hospital the previous day—evidence of recent memory, too.

Several incidents during this visit caused Moshe merriment. A piece of cucumber falling out of the baby's mouth made him roar with laughter. The reaction was out of proportion, but it was apparent that he had the capacity to be amused. Later, he refused to eat a particular orange. When Alon tasted it and said, "I see why you aren't eating it —it's sour," Moshe laughed again.

Moshe was still not eating enough, and Alon warned him that Mrs. Nathan would have to reinsert the nasogastric tube unless he ate more. Yet Moshe continued to refuse food. Before the operation I had been fighting a losing battle against Moshe's overeating. Now I was at a loss to help him put some of this weight back. What a topsy-turvy world it had become!

# ❖ ❖ ❖ 22 ❖ ❖ ❖
## Experts

The time had come to call in specialists from other departments. Sixteen weeks after Moshe's surgery, Dr. Margolis, head of the only rehabilitation unit in Jerusalem, at Hadassah Hospital, came to see him at the request of Dr. Benson, who had twice visited Moshe in the chronic geriatric unit.

Dr. Benson had discussed with me transferring Moshe to Bet Levenstein, a hospital said to have the greatest experience with neurologically damaged patients. But Bet Levenstein is near Tel Aviv, about ninety minutes by car from Jerusalem. Neither my children nor I would be able to visit Moshe daily there. I asked Dr. Ramin, the chief clinical psychologist at Bet Levenstein, whether their work with brain-damaged patients warranted such a partial separation. Dr. Ramin strongly advised against transferring Moshe out of Jerusalem, realizing that close contact with family was crucial for his rehabilitation.

At our suggestion, Dr. Margolis addressed Moshe in English. Moshe was able to give his name and profession but he could not tell Dr. Margolis where he was. He raised his right arm upon request but was unable to differentiate between "up" and "down" and suffered from "neglect" of his left side; that is to say, he seemed unaware of that side. Dr. Margolis felt that Moshe was not yet able to follow instructions to a sufficient degree to be admitted to the Hadassah rehabilitation unit. Moshe would also have to become aware of the left side of his body in order to be admitted.

To further Moshe's progress, especially mental processes, such as thinking and remembering, Dr. Margolis suggested that we stimulate him in diverse ways. He recommended that we bring Moshe books and photographs that he particularly liked, show him newspapers, play cassettes of his favorite music, and, above all, talk to him about events in his past. Dr. Margolis especially favored home visits in order to arouse memories associated with Moshe's familiar surroundings.

But he also warned us to practice moderation lest we tax Moshe beyond his capacity and thereby evoke a defensive response.

We worried that once Moshe had met the necessary criteria he would have to join the six weeks' waiting list for the rehabilitation unit. But Dr. Margolis assured us that when that time came he would advance Moshe to the head of the list since he had suffered two major traumas, one in relation to his heart and the other in relation to his brain. Little could we guess then that events would ultimately take a different turn.

That same afternoon, as if realizing what was required of him, Moshe complained of an itch on his *left* side.

At lunchtime that day Moshe was also examined by Dr. Ilan, the head of psychiatry at Shaare Zedek Medical Center, whom I knew as a warm and sympathetic colleague. He had earlier offered me his assistance whenever needed. I now asked him for a psychiatric evaluation with a view to helping accelerate Moshe's recovery.

The examination, at which both Alon and I were present, was conducted in Hebrew with Moshe lying in bed. Dr. Ilan asked whether he taught at the university, to which Moshe replied: "Unfortunately."

"Why are you in the hospital?"

"They decided to put me here. They invented the operation as an 'illness.'"

Dr. Ilan enquired what Moshe taught and was told "Semitics." Asked to enumerate some of these languages, Moshe could think only of Ugaritic and maintained that there were no others. But he correctly defined Onkelos as an Aramaic Targum (Bible translation). Dr. Ilan injected a personal note at this point and told Moshe that as a young student he had hated Rashi (the most famous biblical commentator). Moshe reacted drily with, "That's *your* problem. I have other problems."

When Dr. Ilan asked Moshe if he was able to see the flowers in the vase, he replied, "The wonder is that I see."

Throughout this interview Moshe cried a lot, and Dr. Ilan perceived him to be very depressed. He therefore recommended antidepressant medication, which he felt would help Moshe to integrate his experiences. The family had earlier requested that Moshe be taken off Meleril, an antidepressant drug that had been prescribed for him in the acute geriatric ward. Alon objected vehemently to Dr. Ilan's recommendation, since he considered Moshe's emotional reaction totally appropriate. Moreover, he was afraid of unpredictable side effects of the medication. He believed that Moshe's brain could heal without the help of drugs, as it had done up to now, in spite of the doctors' dire predictions. In this belief Alon was supported by Janshi, another psychiatrist, who had visited Moshe frequently during his coma and saw no advantage in giving him antidepressants now. He felt that Moshe was progressing remarkably well.

"Why are you so certain that Meleril should not be prescribed?" Dr. Ilan asked Alon.

"I am quite comfortable with my own stand," Alon replied without elaborating.

"If I had a father in such a condition, I would give him this mediation," Dr. Ilan said, and left the room.

I shared Alon's reasoning, so Moshe was not given antidepressant drugs.

This discussion had been conducted in Moshe's presence. He now turned to Alon and said, "You have a special approach in these matters because you understand and see things differently than other people." It seemed as if his old perspicacity was coming through again. Then, bursting into tears, he added, "Alon helps us." Later he complained, "I don't want different people giving different answers." Multiple opinions seemed to confuse him—he was not yet able to cope with choices.

When he next visited Moshe, Dr. Ilan drew my attention to his numerous wisecracks and puns, which, although sometimes clever and funny, were mostly facetious. For example, when I told Moshe that I wanted to see him walk with a cane, he said, "Yes, citizen." When I asked him whether he had his hanky, he answered, "Yes, hanky-panky." Dr. Ilan suggested that Moshe had *Witzelsucht* (joking disease). I was unaware that a hundred years ago the famous neurologist Hughlings Jackson had recognized this as a fundamental form of nervous "dissolution."* In this state, due either to a presumed frontal-

*For more on *Witzelsucht*, see "Yes, Father-Sister" in Oliver Sacks, *The Man Who Mistook His Wife for a Hat* (1987, pp. 116–119) and J. Taylor, ed., *Selected Writings of John Hughlings Jackson* (1931, reprint 1958).

lobe syndrome (or to schizophrenia), there ceases to be any "center" to the mind. Other psychiatrists and neurologists had also hypothesized that Moshe's lack of inhibition (disinhibition syndrome) was due to frontal-lobe injury. All I knew was that Moshe had always been an inveterate punster—hence this kind of joking did not seem to me unusual or abnormal. My ignorance of *Witzelsucht* spared me a fear which, in any case, turned out to be unfounded.

❖

The neurologist Dr. Varon introduced himself as Moshe was finishing his lunch. Moshe burped loudly, and Dr. Varon asked me if he had behaved in that way prior to his illness. Dr. Varon was obviously unaware not only of Moshe's German upbringing but also of the fact that he was a professor.

I was sorry that I had been requested to leave the room while Dr. Varon and Dr. Frisch, the psychiatrist, examined Moshe. Dr. Varon told me later that Moshe was suffering from serious brain damage, especially of the frontal lobes. He wanted to take Moshe into his department for further observation. But at that time neurology functioned only on an outpatient basis, so there were no neurological beds. (Who were the main losers, I wondered, Moshe or the neurologists?)*

We rejected Dr. Varon's recommendation for narcoanalysis—a neuropsychiatric examination that involves the administration of a narcotic. Feeling strongly that Moshe was finally recovering slowly from his coma, we did not want to allow the doctors to induce a stuporous state in him, even if only temporarily.

*Unhappily the notes of both Dr. Varon and Dr. Ilan had disappeared from the hospital records when I requested to see them for this book.

# ❖ ❖ ❖ 23 ❖ ❖ ❖

# "This Hand Doesn't Belong to Me"

Words tend to be used by certain disciplines in a very specific way. I became aware of this when Dr. Margolis said that Moshe suffered from neglect of his left side. To neurologists, *neglect* means that the brain has failed altogether to register the presence of a certain part of the body, not that the person is simply ignoring that part.

How did Dr. Margolis reach the conclusion that Moshe suffered from "neglect"? When he asked Moshe to raise his left arm, Moshe did not react in any way, though he did raise his right arm on request. Nor did he respond when he was asked to cross his right leg over his left. It seemed that Moshe lacked all awareness of the left side of his body. He had lost the representation of that side in the brain.

The impairment was located in the brain. It is the opposite of a "phantom limb," a persistent image of part of the body, generally a limb, following its loss (usually due to amputation). The brain continues to acknowledge the limb despite its absence.

Moshe experienced the alienation from his left limbs although they had not been injured. In spite of Moshe's reacting to touch, pain, and change of temperature in these limbs, they felt foreign and lifeless to him.

Two days after Dr. Margolis's visit, during lunch, Moshe pushed some crumbs away with his left hand. I pointed to the hand and asked which one it was. He replied, "This hand doesn't belong to me." It appeared that he had completely disowned his left hand, experiencing it as if it were part of a foreign body.

Two days later Moshe complained of having cold hands and asked me to warm them for him. He was clearly aware of having a left and a right hand, but he referred to the left hand as "the dead one." Moreover, his awareness of his left side was unstable; a few days later he referred to his left hand as "my shit right hand" and "the other right hand." But at least he was using a personal pronoun in relation to his left hand—he was beginning to own it.

Exactly four months after Moshe's coronary bypass, Dr. Varon, the neurologist, asked him where his left hand was. Moshe:

"It got lost."

"And your right hand?"

"It exists."

Yet Moshe was able to point to his left hand on request. So progression and regression as usual proceeded alternately.

Three days later Moshe complained that his left foot was dead; he claimed that it did not function because "it did not want to," even though he walked more steadily than ever with the help of a walker. He was now using his left hand to tilt the soup plate, cutting his meat with both hands (although unwillingly), and opening cans using the left hand to steady them. He pushed his peas onto the spoon with his left forefinger and held onto the basin with his left hand while brushing his teeth with the right one. When the doctor asked him to raise his left arm he did so, adding jokingly, "Heil Hitler."

In occupational therapy and physiotherapy, Moshe was willing to follow instructions with both hands, whereas before he had refused to do exercises that involved his left hand. For example, he could pick up a key with his left hand and throw it. Yet all the while he complained that his left hand was cold and dead, that it had been "killed."

Another ten days elapsed. We were sitting in the hospital plaza. Moshe did not want me to sit on the left bench, "because the left is not good for us."

The problem showed itself in all its intensity when the physiotherapist asked him to turn left one day. Moshe turned full circle to the right until he arrived at the designated spot on his left.

❖

I was recently fascinated by Dr. Oliver Sacks's description of Mrs. S. in "Eyes Right," a chapter of his book *The Man Who Mistook His Wife for a Hat* (1987). This patient, who had suffered a massive stroke affecting the deeper and back portions of her right cerebral hemisphere, had totally lost the concept *left*. Unlike Moshe, she could not even look left directly. Like him she could not turn left; she could only turn right through a circle. Sacks terms this disability *hemi-inattention* and *left hemi-field extinction.* \*

❖ ❖ ❖ 24 ❖ ❖ ❖

## Other Impairments

Four months after the coronary bypass, the doctor announced to Moshe that he was going to have a CAT scan. Moshe complained, "My head got lost" (*harosh avood*). He was obviously aware that something was terribly wrong with him.

The brain scan showed damage in the right parietal, temporal, and frontal lobes. This explained Moshe's aggression as well as his problems with numbers and spatial orientation. Trauma to the brain such as that sustained by Moshe affects not only specific areas but the surrounding neural connections as well.

Moshe also had an EEG at this time, which pointed to a general disturbance with a more specific inability to organize and synthesize data.

Moshe had great difficulty in orienting himself in space. He could not find his way around his ward. He could not remember which way to turn from the physiotherapy room in order to get to the dining area, though he took that short walk every day. Nor did he recollect in which direction the bathroom at home lay. In fact, he tended to choose the wrong direction.

Moshe also had a problem with numbers. He could not remember his birthday or the birthdays of people close to him. He did not know how old he or any of us were. He guessed wildly. Watching one of

---

*For more on left-sided neglect or spatial agnosia, see A. R. Luria, *The Working Brain: An Introduction to Neuropsychology* (1973, pp. 165–166) and M. M. Mesulam, *Principles of Behavioral Neurology* (1985, pp. 259–288).

the home movies, he guessed that Alon was eight years old and that Jonathan, who is three and a half years younger, was eight or ten years old. He gave baby Elisha's age as ten years and did not know how long he and I had been married. He often covered up for his deficits by maintaining that he was only fooling or by giving vague answers.

He could not read the time correctly on the new analog watch I had bought him to replace the stolen one, and he was unable to do addition, subtraction, or division, although he remembered the multiplication tables. About three weeks after regaining consciousness he cooperated with Jonathan in practicing these skills.

It was clear that Moshe would have to relearn dates, phone numbers, the evaluation of time, and arithmetic skills.

Moshe progressed quickly. Four weeks after coming out of the coma, he knew the day of the week and the age of our older son. When told the date and that it was somebody's birthday, he guessed correctly that it was Alon's birthday. He also read the time on his analog watch. An apt pupil!

Moshe had another symptom frequently associated with brain damage: he suffered from perseveration, the persistent repetition of an activity. The patient suffering from this syndrome acts like a scratched phonograph record. In his speech Moshe would cling to a topic, particularly one that upset him. He seemed unable to let go of it in spite of the arguments of the person with whom he talked. It was therefore often difficult to have a serious discussion with him.

His recollection of past events appeared excellent. He remembered the names of people from his past as well as their characteristics, and said mockingly to a friend, "Mr. Webber, you were an orthodox Jew once." He recalled long Hebrew prayers and biblical quotations so well that he could change a particular word to suit his needs. For example, when Alon quoted from the first chapter of Isaiah in Hebrew: "Children have I reared and brought up," Moshe continued, also in Hebrew, "And they have *not* rebelled against me," showing Alon by the addition of the word *not* that he appreciated his filial behavior.

But above all, he remembered all his former languages. He spoke to us in German, English, and Hebrew, answered Yiddish and Arab speakers in their own tongues, and quoted or reacted to French, Italian, and Latin sayings.

However, there were problems with Moshe's short-term memory. He told me that he had not eaten lunch when I knew that he had. He became furious when I did not believe him and demanded that I get him some lunch.

Although we had often told him that he was at the Shaare Zedek Medical Center, he believed he was at the university. I would correct him, yet half an hour later he would again maintain that he was at the university, not in a hospital. We were not sure whether he was failing to *learn* the information—perhaps it was too painful to absorb—or failing to *retain* it. It took him three weeks to learn and retain this piece of information.

He retained other items more quickly. He remembered that I was going to a concert with my mother a short while after I told him so. Frequently he told me the names of people who had visited him hours or days earlier. He also remembered the names of all the nurses and orderlies.

Moshe could not remember anything about his coma or the three weeks preceding his surgery, during which he was hospitalized in the intensive coronary unit. His last recollection was of coming home from the theater and experiencing great difficulty walking. However, there were two major exceptions to this retrograde amnesia. Shlomo, a nurse in the intensive coronary unit when Moshe was there, was transferred to the chronic geriatric ward shortly after Moshe awoke from his coma. Moshe recognized him, recalled his name, and said, "from the heart" (i.e., the coronary unit). He also remembered Naama's and Shlomi's wedding, which he attended eleven days before his operation.

Dr. Varon, the neurologist, was unable to predict whether Moshe's brain damage would be permanent, but he held out hope that the problems would decrease in time.

The psychologist who had tested Moshe over several days found that his spatial ability had been badly affected; he scored only 1 on the Wechsler Blocks Design test.* I remembered that Moshe, on ar-

---

*This is a subtest of the Wechsler Adult Intelligence test. The subject has to reproduce seven geometric designs with sixteen cubes. To do this, he or she has to analyze the whole into its component parts and then synthesize them. Scores on this subtest range from a low of 1 to a high of 10.

riving in Tokyo for the first time, had (with the help of a map), driven to the hotel as if he were a long-time resident of the city. I had always been the one who could not read maps or find my way around new places.

The psychologist also informed me that Moshe had problems with concentration, which she thought impeded his arithmetic ability, as well as learning and retaining new information. She attributed these deficits to damage in the frontal and parietal lobes of the brain. Moshe's previous knowledge and comprehension remained relatively unaffected. On the Wechsler Adult Intelligence test there was a large discrepancy between Moshe's score on the Performance Scale (61) and the Verbal Scale (88).* His scores indicated that he had not achieved his former level of intelligence. The psychologist did notice occasional sparks of brilliance in Moshe, however, hinting at his former superior cognitive level.

Moshe felt very helpless and angry about his poor achievement on the tests. He even cried when he could not answer one of the psychologist's questions.

Since Moshe's general knowledge, social understanding, and ability to abstract were still reasonably good, and since his functioning had improved since awakening from the coma, the psychologist considered the test results as a baseline, implying that further rehabilitation would lead to improvement.

She suggested that we refamiliarize Moshe with significant dates like birthdays and anniversaries and that we indicate directions verbally. She thought it more effective to say, "The bathroom is on the left" than to show Moshe a map, which would only frustrate him.

Although I was aware of Moshe's tremendous progress since he

*The five subtests comprising the Performance Scale are: Picture Arrangement (measuring the ability to comprehend a total situation), Picture Completion (measuring the ability to differentiate essential from unessential details), Block Design (described above), Digit Symbol (measuring the ability to associate symbols), and Object Assembly (which tells something about the subject's mode of perception). The five subtests comprising the Verbal Scale are: Information, Comprehension, Memory Test for Digits (forward and backward), Similarities, and Arithmetic Reasoning. All subtests are scored on a scale of 1 to 10, 1 being the lowest. The final scores are similar to IQ scores, in which 100 is considered average.

had awakened from his coma, I found the psychologist's evaluation very upsetting, since the scores were so drastically below Moshe's former level of intelligence: on the Performance Scale he scored as a mental defective while on the Verbal Scale he scored as a dull normal. The psychologist suggested a retest in six months' time, but by then Moshe was no longer willing to serve as a test subject.

## ❖ ❖ ❖ 25 ❖ ❖ ❖
# "They Announced I Am Dead"

I had seldom seen Moshe in such anguish. The son-in-law of one of the patients in his room took me aside when I arrived to tell me that his father-in-law had died during the night. The nurse had tried to hide this fact from Moshe in order not to upset him. They had wheeled the dead man out in his own bed, as if he were merely being taken for some tests. Only later had they informed Moshe about the death.

Moshe seemed completely confused when I arrived. "I had a terrible day fighting the establishment," he told me. "The establishment is not set up for dead people. The people next to me are dead. They sent a man in, announcing death. I complained." When I wondered why he complained, he screamed, "Because they didn't announce death. Terrible event. They announced I am dead." Moshe had been so close to death himself that he was not sure even now whether he was alive or dead. As far as he was concerned any death could be his own.

I did my best to reason with him while he was having his meal.

"You can't be dead if you are eating," I argued.

But Moshe was adamant: "Last night when it happened it was terrible. I expected you to hear the announcement that I am dead."

I tried to be logical. "But you are breathing and talking—only live people are capable of that."

"You have no understanding."

How could I understand Moshe's dreadful fear? I had not realized that he could so closely identify with another person as to believe that he shared his fate. Or was he unable to differentiate between himself and others? Alon told me that Moshe had been convinced that everyone in his room had died. Alon attempted to convince him that the other patient was still alive, but Moshe maintained that his two fellow patients were one and the same and therefore both were dead.

Once again it became clear to me that telling even a painful truth is preferable to withholding it, in spite of the best intentions of the person who suppresses it, though I cannot be sure that Moshe would have been spared his fear even if he had been told the truth immediately.

# ❖ ❖ ❖ 26 ❖ ❖ ❖
## Changing Relations

Gradually Moshe's feelings toward me and others became more ambivalent—no longer merely abusive. Thus, one day, he greeted me with: "Good morning, Mummy." Yet when I asked how he was, he replied, "Damn you."

Another day, after he had cursed me and declared that he wanted a different wife, he added, "Mummy, good food." (They say the way to a man's heart is through his stomach!)

When Moshe complained about women, Alon explained, "If it weren't for Mummy you wouldn't be around." Moshe replied, "Could be," and then agreed with Alon that I am a good mother. He even pleaded with Alon to "be decent to her." So gradually he was admitting more of my positive qualities.

Bayla visited Moshe weekly. Sixteen weeks after surgery, he told her that he did not like me, adding, "She's not good for you."

Bayla replied, "I like her and want to be her friend anyhow."

"You understand," Moshe responded. However, a little while later he told her, "You are an idiot."

Bayla countered this with "I am smart"; whereupon Moshe cried: "Thank you for being smart."

Rachel, his devoted assistant, realized that whenever Moshe did not feel understood, he would curse. So she suggested that she try to guess what he meant. He agreed to this idea but added, "Guess intelligently." He was now identifying several people—including Lazer, the orderly, and his assistants, Shraga and Rachel—by name, to their delight. But he frequently called Alon "Elisha" and me "Plussy"—which had become the generic name for members of our immediate family. He called for Plussy often during the day. When told that Jonathan had exams that prevented him from coming right away, Moshe said that the exams didn't interest him. He was obviously not yet the Moshe he used to be, whose primary concern had been that the boys complete their studies as soon as possible.

Moshe was now even more insistent that I stay with him. "I want you to be here," he cried to me; "I hate to be without you." One day I told him I had to go see my mother. "Tell her not to take time from me," he objected. Once I tried to assuage his anger at my leaving by telling him that Alon would be there soon. "Alon is no substitute for you," he responded. This reaction reminded me of the separation anxiety of a toddler, who cries whenever his mother leaves the room and refuses to accept a substitute.

Yet this need for me could suddenly be turned into "I don't want anybody. I don't want you." Moshe resorted to name-calling and cursing when I did not understand what he wanted. Conversational topics frequently made him irritable. When I enquired whether he had gone to synagogue at the hospital on Saturday morning, he replied, "As if you had anything to do with synagogue; you don't." He found reasons to quarrel with me even about topics he imagined were being discussed. "It's ridiculous for somebody grown-up to talk about money," he said once, when I had done nothing of the kind.

At times Moshe seemed intent on insulting me. He spoke about my "so-called patients." He also took more cognizance of my note-taking and made derogatory remarks about it. He referred to "the dirt" I was

writing and maintained that I was incapable of writing anything better. He even accused me of "copying for the eightieth time," adding,
"Alon is ten times better than you." He was clearly trying to play me
against my own son.

I realized what was happening and merely smiled at these insults.
I knew that just as there can be no light without shadow, so there can
be no love without hate or resentment. For Moshe the shadow was
still taking the upper hand a good deal of the time.

I offered to show Moshe my notes about his illness, but he did
not want to see them. He mockingly referred to my note-taking as
"Wissenschaft" (science) and said he could not stand it. "Whatever I
have is being misinterpreted," he complained. I learned to take notes
when he was not looking. He later told Yona that he had made me
stop taking notes. I suppose he did not want to be the object of any
study.

Moshe was intolerant of my slightest failings and overreacted to
each of them. When he received a slight blow as I brought his wheelchair too close to the dining-room table, he complained that I was
breaking his bones.

He was liable to change his mind from moment to moment and
with it the feelings directed at me. One evening he was dissatisfied
with his supper, and I proposed to supplement the meal with a can
of tuna. "No, I'll throw it on your head," he shouted. Yet a moment
later he quietly asked for the tuna. His rapidly altering moods again
reminded me of the sudden changes of feelings in young children.

❖

Moshe remembered the names and characteristics of old friends soon
after regaining consciousness, and he adapted his talk accordingly.
Uri, a very gentle, well-brought up colleague and friend, visited him
at a time when Moshe was cursing freely. Moshe turned to him at
one point, saying, "*Scheisse* [shit]. You don't know what that means."
He implied that Uri was too refined to understand such language.
Perhaps he even wanted to provoke Uri with his curses. But he repeatedly thanked him for coming to see him, as if trying to match
Uri's good behavior.

When Moshe became aware that his assistants were visiting him
during their working hours, he told me, "I don't want these people

to give up their working hours for which I am paying. I want them to work on the Bible project. I don't want visitors." His work was becoming a primary consideration for him again only two weeks after he had regained full consciousness.

His old tendency to be sarcastic now reappeared. A doctor who inquired how he felt got the reply, "Great, couldn't be better."

But Moshe could also be pleasant and considerate. For instance, when Mrs. Nathan fixed him a sandwich, he exclaimed, "You are wonderful!" To her inquiry whether she should make him some tea, he replied, "If that is not too much bother."

❖ ❖ ❖ 27 ❖ ❖ ❖
## "I'm Still Alive—I Want to Live"

October 20: the third home visit took place without an attendant orderly. Only eight days out of coma, Moshe had come a long way. As he sat down for lunch with us, he wished me *bon appétit* in Hebrew but objected to my praising the soup—he did not want me to give grades to the food I had prepared. He asked my mother if she had enough food. I was delighted that he was beginning to show concern for other people.

After lunch Moshe lay down to rest, wearing earplugs to eliminate all noise. When he woke up, he announced, "I am still alive—I want to live." I was overjoyed. This was Moshe's first positive, existential statement. At long last he had come out in favor of life. He now asked where I was and whether I existed as if to emphasize his need for my support in his battle to return to life.

Moshe shaved himself for the first time, using his electric shaver. Alon then gave him a pen and paper and asked him to write: "Hubs-pups [our term of endearment for Moshe] loves everyone." did so in handwriting that was similar to his former script, though the words flowed into each other, the *e* was missing from *loves,* and the letters of the last word got progressively smaller. But knowing the message, we were able to decipher the writing easily. So Moshe had not forgotten how to write. We had good reason to be grateful!

When the phone rang, Moshe lifted the receiver and said "Erev Tov" (good evening). It was Marvin calling from Boston to inquire about Moshe's progress. Without identifying himself, he expressed his delight at hearing Moshe's voice. Later, Marvin asked Alon, "Does your father know to whom he talked just now?" Alon repeated the question to Moshe, who reacted with, "You idiot, of course I know: Marvin." Hearing this reply, Marvin felt reassured that Moshe was back.

That evening, when Alon drove Moshe back to the hospital, Moshe waved to me. It seemed more and more like old times.

Two days later my heart sank when Moshe reverted to the blasphemous German he had been using when frustrated. Demanding his earplugs, he called on "the holy mother of God." He exclaimed, "Jesus, Maria, and Joseph" and "only Jesus can help us" in relation to some other source of limitation. The young German orderly was rather shocked by Moshe's curses. When he called on Jesus, she asked him if he had been a professor of religious studies. She could not imagine how else he would know all these profanities.

Moshe's irritativeness and impatience were exacerbated by lack of sufficient sleep. He constantly complained of fatigue. Sleeping pills were ineffective in prolonging his sleep. He told his friend Chaim Tadmor that he did not want to give in to his fatigue and sleep during the day lest he be unable to sleep at night. Such reasoning demonstrated that he was able to predict the consequence of an act and plan for the future.

Nothing seemed right to Moshe when he was tired. He ordered me around and regressed to using anal language. Moshe expressed his impatience via exaggeration such as "I told you thirty times" and "I asked you five thousand times for a drink."

My concern and caring for him as expressed through food—I was always with him when he ate his lunch—obviously annoyed him. "Will you please stop playing grandmother?" he requested. "Why do you have to serve me?" Clearly, he wanted to be independent.

Yet he also got angry with me when I refused to cut his meat since he was quite capable of doing it himself. Occasionally he ate it uncut and smiled at me like a naughty boy who knows he is breaking the rules. On one such occasion, I remarked that it was easier to eat meat after cutting it. He reacted with his usual aggression: "Shall I cut your nose?" I should have left well enough alone.

He was hypersensitive to what he experienced as my instructing him. "Stop teaching me." I felt he wanted to be my equal as in days gone by.

Four weeks out of coma, Moshe was still prone to tears whenever he was upset or excited. When he overheard me telling Tamara about a woman who had lost her twin babies soon after their birth, he shed tears as he said, "Tote Kinder" (dead children). He started weeping after guessing correctly that it was Alon's twenty-ninth birthday and also when I told him about *Heimat*, a German film I enjoyed. A week later, he heard another patient who was being interviewed by a doctor talk about death. Reporting this to me, he cried and said in Hebrew: "It was emotional" (*meragesh*). He could not elaborate—the subject seemed too loaded. He also wept profusely when he wrote his first letter about recent events to Gershon.

❖

The phone rang at home. I was excited to hear Moshe's voice at the other end with "Hi, Mummy." He had asked an orderly to dial our number on the public pay phone. Here was a new bridge built between home and hospital only three weeks after he recovered consciousness. Moshe used the phone whenever he felt bored or upset about not having visitors, although he could not remember our phone number.

About a week later he phoned at 8:00 A.M. Where was I? he wanted to know. I usually arrived at the hospital around ten, but apparently Moshe did not realize that. He told me that my friend Batya had "defended" me when he tried unsuccessfully to get me on the phone "all morning." He was upset because no orderly had come to his bed when he called. So he had gotten out of bed by himself. I shared with him my fear that he might fall and hurt himself. "That's what I also thought," was his reply.

I thought that the phone might help to reawaken his interest in work, so I suggested that he call his colleagues at the Bible project.

"I don't want to hear about that," he screamed. In fact there was a lot he did not want to hear about, such as the names of visitors, the very mention of which he considered "loathsome." But a few days later, when the head of the Institute for Jewish Studies asked if he wanted to visit the institute, Moshe delightedly asked when he could go. And he turned to his assistants, Rachel and Shraga, with "Tell me what is happening at the Bible project." They were overjoyed to inform him about developments there.

The "unfreezing" of Moshe's memory also proceeded apace. When told that Nahum, a friend and colleague, had called, he said, correctly, "From Boston." He addressed his colleagues by their names. His old word associations re-emerged. As he started away from me one day, I asked where he was going. "To a place of worms" (*limkom reema vetole'a*)—that is, the grave—he answered in Hebrew, with a big smile. He was quoting from the funeral prayers, which include the sentence "Know where you are going" and continue with the words Moshe had used. Similarly, when I called "See you later" on my way out, he responded, "Thank God you didn't say 'alligator' "—alluding to a piece of family banter we used when our boys were small.

A nurse's arrival to take blood for a test set him off on a recitation of the list of the ten plagues: "Blood, frogs . . ." It was as if he were programmed to recite whole chains of words associated with a specific word.

At around this time he became able to piece together several details of his past with the help of his long-term memory:

"Where were you born?"

Moshe answered correctly, "Berlin."

"Where did you go from there?"

"England." This was incorrect—he had gone to Israel.

"When did you come here?"

Moshe preferred an imprecise answer: "A long time ago."

"Do you know any languages apart from English and Hebrew?"

"That's enough."

For most people two languages really are enough, but not for Moshe, who that very day not only spoke in German, English, and Hebrew but also said in French, referring to a certain drink, "Ce n'est pas potable" (this is not drinkable).

I continued my questions: "Where do you teach?"

"Hebrew University."

"What subject?"

"Semitics."

Moshe still did not know dates. He was completely wrong about the length of our marriage and appeared ignorant of Jonathan's age (but he covered up by saying, "Too old"). He did not even know his own age, although when I reminded him that he had had a birthday in the hospital, he remembered that it was his sixtieth.

His memory for recent events showed signs of improvement. He now knew the names of the nurses, referring to the head nurse as "the boss." When Chaim Tadmor wondered whether Moshe had been at home that day, Moshe answered correctly that he had visited home the previous day, adding, "I have a loving family." When Chaim gave him "regards from Jonas," Moshe replied, "He was here a few days ago."

He was beginning to realize more facts about his current situation. Asked if he knew where he was, he replied: "Wallach," the former name of Shaare Zedek Medical Center. He told people that he had had a chest operation and looked at his scar.

Moshe now came home twice weekly. At his fourth visit, he asked, "Is there a place for me at the table or is it usurped?" As if I had sensed his fear of being supplanted, I had not allowed anyone to sit in his seat throughout the five months of his hospitalization. When Jonathan saw Moshe's empty chair at the dinner table that first Friday evening when Moshe lay in the intensive coronary unit, he had burst into tears. The empty chair seemed to symbolize for him Moshe's absence.

But in another sense, Moshe's place had been usurped. Had I not, with the help of the boys, gradually taken over most of the functions within the home? And did I not now see myself as solely responsible for the household, able to make decisions concerning home and family without consulting Moshe? It would require concerted effort and determination on my part to reassign a significant place within the family to Moshe. I felt in the same position as wives of prisoners of war or of men missing in action, whose husbands return after a prolonged period of absence during which it is not known whether they would return. These women had assumed their husbands' responsibilities, but once the men were back, the women reverted to their original roles.

During this visit, Moshe expressed his appreciation at being home. He held Elisha on his lap and talked to him.

Yona phoned Moshe at home and he teased her: "How come you carry on with strange men?" (meaning Jonathan). "I am marrying your son," she replied. "Unbelievable," he said.

On his fifth home visit, Moshe arrived with a walker instead of the wheelchair. He was no longer so dependent on other people.

Alon read a letter to him that I had received from Professor Urbach, head of the World Congress of Jewish Studies, announcing Moshe's reappointment to the presidium of the association. Moshe cried with excitement at the news. I felt that Professor Urbach had written the letter to instill in me the hope that one day Moshe would be well enough to take on his erstwhile duties. To Moshe it no doubt meant that he had not been dropped.

The following day, three weeks after he came out of his coma, Moshe looked at the newspaper he held in his lap. I was not sure how much of it he took in. When I asked him about a news item, the students' strike, Moshe maintained that that was "nothing new." I wondered whether that phrase, which he used whenever he did not want to hear or read news, was a coverup allowing him to avoid coping with the media.

❖ ❖ ❖ 28 ❖ ❖ ❖
## Slow Return

Moshe showed an ever increasing interest in family events. This went hand in hand with a diminution of his self-centeredness.

His old spirit was coming back, especially with people he liked a lot. For instance, when Ruth, an old friend and the wife of a coworker, brought him regards from David, I asked him if he knew which David: "Maybe King David?" "Her king," he replied. Later, she took her leave and promised to visit him again soon. "Durchaus erwünscht" (absolutely desired), he said.

He seemed able to say what people wanted to hear and apparently wished to please them. On the phone he told Tamara that he was not feeling well because he missed his "daughter" Tamara.

She argued: "But you have your son with you."

"That isn't good enough."

To Yona he said, "I haven't given you my mazel tov wishes yet" (congratulations on her engagement to Jonathan), and he gave her the kiss she requested.

He was relearning the social graces. Rodney examined Moshe during one of his home visits because he had complained of pains. Moshe thanked Rodney profusely. He told my mother, "Please don't forget to say thank you to Werner" (Werner had given him suspenders to hold up his pants, now far too large for him). To a friend of Alon who had visited him, Moshe said, "Nice meeting you." And he expressed his appreciation when his friends came to see him. Gone was the abusive talk about them.

He was altogether more aware of the effect he had on other people and voiced his feeling that even though his assistants thought he was an idiot, he thought his intelligence was better than ever. Yet his self-assurance was highly unstable. That same day, when his friend and colleague Chaim Rabin visited him, Moshe cried, "I am a useless man." Another time he referred to his "verdrehtes Kopf" (screwed-up head).

More and more he blamed the doctors for his condition. "The doctors have you in their hands," he said, "and you don't realize it. They killed me, they exploded the vein" (referring to the scar on the leg).

At this time his verbal aggression tended to be directed mainly to our sons and me. He still became furious and shouted at us when something did not go as he expected. But positive feelings for me were more pronounced now. He called out with joy across the corridor when he saw me arrive one morning and was very affectionate when it was time for me to leave, even though he had screamed at me earlier because I did not understand what he wanted me to do.

Whenever he was alone he phoned Tamara and me, asking where we were. He felt he needed us close to him, particularly since he did not know what to do with his time.

Moshe continued to become more aware of his environment. He stated plainly that he did not want to be in the hospital and cried as he told a friend, "You don't know how terrible it is to be here. It is so degrading." The comforting words Mrs. Nathan had spoken when I was wavering about consenting to Moshe's transfer to the chronic geriatric unit now rang in my ears: "Your husband is unaware of his surroundings. As soon as he becomes aware of them, he'll leave for the rehabilitation unit." At least Moshe's suffering on account of his surroundings was evidence of significant progress.

Moshe was tied to his wheelchair so that he would not slide down or fall out. He complained of being "on the leash." He wanted me rather than "strangers" to get him out of bed and help him in the toilet. He could not grasp the fact that I was unable to do this unaided.

On his sixth home visit, three weeks after regaining consciousness, Moshe wanted to go out. With his walker he walked half the way to the Laromme Hotel restaurant, a block from our home. The rest of the way we wheeled him in his wheelchair.

Sitting at the table, surrounded by his family, he looked no different from the other hotel guests. No one would have guessed that he had only recently "returned to life." He even made appropriate small talk. I showed him pictures of Yona and Jonathan's engagement party, which had been held while he was still in a coma, and pointed out how attractive Yona's mother, Miriam, was. "Like her daughter," he said.

He was starting to make plans for a future in which he envisioned himself as healthy. He told Jonathan that he would like to go to a hotel once he was well, "if we have the money." Jonathan responded that Moshe had savings, whereupon Moshe hushed him, as if this were a secret.

Yet in spite of progress in many areas, Moshe still seemed confused at times. He asked whether I had met Yona's father in my hotel and became angry with me for not knowing which hotel he meant. "How stupid you are—where we all had dinner a week ago," he snapped.

"Do you think I live there?"

"I don't know where you live," said Moshe.

I told him the name of our street.

"Perhaps," he grumbled.

On the way to his seventh home visit, Moshe got up and out of his wheelchair, seated himself in the car, and closed the car door unaided.

❖ ❖ ❖ 29 ❖ ❖ ❖

## Literacy

In the first three weeks after awakening, Moshe demonstrated to us that he had retained his ability to read and write. He had read "Ich liebe Dich" in printed letters (even before regaining full consciousness), a Hebrew menu card, and part of a Hebrew newspaper; he had written an English sentence dictated to him by Alon.

We followed this up by bringing him some of his published articles —but he refused to look at them. Yossi asked him if they were too difficult for him to read. He denied it vehemently, adding that the papers were by his students, to whom he had suggested the ideas. Actually they were his own articles, but we were gratified that he still took pride in the scholarship he had transmitted to others.

Abigail, our sixteen-year-old niece from Los Angeles, wrote Moshe a charming letter in the form of a story about their relationship. She wrote that at the time of her birth he reportedly said, "At long last I will have someone to look after me in my old age." This had become an oft-quoted family joke. Moshe wept when he saw her letter. I asked if he wanted me to read it to him. He protested that he was old enough to read. For the first time, I was certain that he was reading a text in longhand. He was adamant that I should not read or even touch the letter, like a little boy with a new toy.

Would Moshe ever again be able to compose a text of his own? The opportunity to find out came about four weeks after he regained

consciousness. He was once again grumbling about his physiotherapist, Adina. Mrs. Nathan jokingly suggested that he should complain
to the management about her and gave him a pen and a sheet of
notepaper. Moshe thereupon wrote his first letter (in Hebrew):

> To the Management of Shaare Zedek Medical Center
> Subject: Murder by Miss Adina G.
> The following complaint is filed in the matter of overwork
> [demanded] by Miss Adina G. who tried to work me too hard
> while I was in treatment. [three undecipherable words follow.]
> Sincerely, The poor suffering Goshen

That Moshe could write tongue in cheek was apparent not only
from the content of the letter but especially from the way he signed
off. The wording throughout was his own. He wrote in his old handwriting, now restored to its former size. "Sincerely" and the signature
were run in with the last sentence, but otherwise he spaced the letter
quite well, though it was not centered on the page. We were absolutely
thrilled with it.

Mrs. Nathan got into the spirit and straightaway wrote the following reply in Hebrew:

> Prof. Goshen,                                                    Nov. 3
> We received your letter of complaint. The subject will be in-
> vestigated. Should it transpire that you were right, the physio-
> therapist will get a prize for her competence. But if your com-
> plaint turns out to be due to your laziness, we will have to draw
> the appropriate consequences and make you work even harder!!
> Good luck,
> Leni Nathan

That same day at home, Moshe read a page of Günter Grass's *Cat
and Mouse* and instantly translated it into English for the non-German
speakers in the room. He had chosen the book, which he might well
have selected in the best of times, from the library cart at the hospital.

Later during the home visit (the seventh), Moshe protested for the
first time about having to return to the hospital. Alon explained that
he was not yet independent enough around the toilet to stay at home.

Thereupon Moshe raised himself from the wheelchair and went with his walker to the toilet. He was obviously determined to prove Alon wrong. His strong motivation was his best ally.

Nevertheless, he cried about what had become of him and maintained that he would never be the person he had been. To re-enter daily life was clearly a tremendous exertion for him, and he required our constant encouragement to persevere in this struggle.

That afternoon, Jonathan tested Moshe's memory by asking him the whereabouts of a particular book in his very large library (the books stand three rows deep). Moshe pointed to the book unhesitatingly. It appeared that his old spatial map had not been eradicated during the coma. But he was still unable to find his way about the ward, presumably because he could not easily construct new spatial engrams (lasting traces in the brain).

Moshe had composed his first humorous letter. What about a more formal letter to a colleague? He tackled this challenge the following day when he decided to express his appreciation in writing to Professor Ephraim Urbach, the president of the World Congress of Jewish Studies, for having reappointed him to the presidium of the association. The only unusual thing about this letter was its placement at the top left of the sheet of paper.

Reading now became a routine activity for Moshe. He perused the front page of the Hebrew newspaper *Ha'aretz* daily.

I was reminded of Dr. Hershkov, our former dental surgeon, who had been hit by a car and had sustained serious brain damage. Like Moshe, he had not remained in a vegetative state, despite his doctors' predictions. But Dr. Hershkov had lost the ability to read and write Hebrew (which was not his mother tongue). He needed a year's intensive training to relearn these skills. "It was like going back to first grade," he told me. He never regained his fluency in reading Hebrew. Hearing his story, I was deeply grateful that Moshe had been spared a similar fate, since Hebrew literacy was so intricately linked to his life's work.

Moshe's main reading was Swift's satire *The Tale of the Tub*, which he had asked me to bring him. When we got him a novel in Hebrew by S. Agnon, one of Moshe's favorite authors (he had known him personally), he maintained that he knew it by heart. This was obviously an excuse to avoid having to read the book. (S. Agnon is the only Israeli Nobel prizewinner in literature.)

To Yona he said one day, "They think I am an idiot and therefore they don't bring me work." This was the signal for Mrs. Nathan to set up a corner of his room—which he shared with two other patients —as a study, with a desk and chair. (She asked him what he liked to have near his desk and he replied, jokingly, "Women.") Shraga and Rachel supplied the necessary books. So, four weeks after awakening from his coma, he sat with Rachel to work on his dictionary. He had asked to be dressed in his suit for the occasion. I blinked half in disbelief at what I saw and heard. Was I dreaming? Rachel had brought index cards containing definitions of words about which she felt uncertain. She now awaited Moshe's verdict about them.

Rachel asked Moshe for the definition of a rarely used Hebrew verb. In reply, he quoted an esoteric hymn by the liturgical poet Elazar Hakalir, incorporating that verb. The hymn is recited only once a year, during the Rosh Hashanah service. Likewise, in response to an unusual adjective, Moshe quoted the Midrash (homiletics) to the book of Genesis, which includes that adjective. These infrequently used words obviously started a chain of verbal associations in Moshe's mind. Later, he produced definitions of words that Rachel read to him.

There were long silences in response to Rachel's questions, but when she asked him after fifteen minutes whether he had had enough, he replied, "To work." To me it appeared only a semblance of work, but Rachel assured me that Moshe not only gave her some correct answers, but also pointed out tautologies and even remembered other contexts in which certain words had occurred. She was pleased to see her boss return to his real specialty.

Rachel sat with Moshe after breakfast twice weekly. On each occasion Moshe's responses came more quickly than the time before. Even I could no longer doubt that he was resuming real work. Moshe gradually increased his working time at the desk to an hour and a half a day. This gave him the feeling that he was back to his former kind of life. I knew from the joyful expression on Rachel's face that she saw significant improvement at each session. She felt that the quality of his work was good, although Moshe's reactions were slower than they had been. He was making a real comeback.

Five weeks after recovering consciousness, Moshe wrote a letter to his group of Targum (Aramaic Bible translation) scholars, whom he had convened from all over the world before he became ill. He expressed his regret for not being able to attend their first meeting and his hope that he would be able to attend the next meeting. On receipt of this letter, representatives of the group visited him in the hospital. Mrs. Nathan set up a room where they could talk undisturbed with Moshe. Moshe joined in the academic small talk and laughed frequently. After they had gone, he phoned to tell me he had had a very exciting meeting with them. The following day he wanted me to get the story from Mrs. Nathan so that I could hear an objective report of this great event, which apparently heralded his return to academic life.

Alon needed help with a long German text for his doctorate. No person was better suited for such an undertaking than Moshe had been before his illness. Would he be up to it now? Alon decided to try him out. For forty-five minutes he read a German theological text to him, and Moshe, in splendid form, helped him understand its full meaning.

### Escape

The president of Bar Ilan University, Professor Rackman, called me one evening in November to ask if he could visit Moshe in the hospital. I was very pleased and arranged for him to come to the hospital on a Tuesday afternoon, at a time when I regularly attend a seminar at the university. I parted with Moshe that Tuesday after lunch, reminding him about his afternoon visitor.

I was surprised when Moshe called me an hour later, complaining that I had invited Professor Rackman without having left Moshe the key. I assured him that no key was required for visitors to enter the hospital. But Moshe was most upset and insisted that he should have a key. I attributed Moshe's worry about a key to his confusion and did not give the matter much further thought.

Imagine my surprise when I returned home from the university and found Moshe, Alon, Tamara, and Mrs. Nathan. The story unfolded: Mrs. Nathan had called Tamara to tell her that "Dad has disappeared." She added that he was last seen strolling with a dignified elderly gentleman who did not at all look like someone who would try to smuggle Moshe out of the hospital. Mrs. Nathan and her staff had searched for Moshe all over the hospital. So had the visitors who had come to see him that afternoon. But there was no trace of him anywhere in the building. Mrs. Nathan was frantic. Alon took the receiver out of Tamara's hand and tried to calm her.

The minute Alon hung up, the phone rang again. Joni, Rodney's wife, informed him that Moshe was at our apartment. Apparently she had heard a loud banging at our door. Moshe had been very angry because he had no key to get into the apartment. Joni, who had a spare key, opened the door for him. She reported that Moshe was accompanied by a distinguished-looking man who left soon after.

Alon immediately phoned Mrs. Nathan and invited her to our apartment, where all of them were assembled when I came home. Moshe smiled sheepishly as they told me the story. Both Mrs. Nathan and Alon told him how worried everyone had been about his disappearance. They impressed on him that he must inform the staff before leaving the hospital.

I was very embarrassed at the idea that Professor Rackman must have thought I was using him as our family driver. Phoning him to apologize, I learned more of the story. As Professor Rackman was getting ready to leave, Moshe asked to be taken home. Professor Rackman took it for granted that Moshe had informed the staff about his plans and saw no need to obtain permission from anyone. He accompanied Moshe to his car, drove to our home, helped Moshe walk up the stairs and rang the bell. Of course no one opened the door. At that point Professor Rackman realized there must have been some mistake.

Moshe had behaved like a naughty, irresponsible child. He was aware of this, and he said apologetically to Mrs. Nathan, "What a mess!" Yet to me he spoke of a "misunderstanding." I believe he was convinced that a university president could be entertained only in one's home, and therefore he had requested the key. I had misinterpreted this request as a sign of his mental confusion.

❖ ❖ ❖ 31 ❖ ❖ ❖

## Reactions to Moshe's Recovery

I fully realized that Moshe had finally emerged from his coma in the face of the enthusiastic reactions of my friends. Some embraced me, weeping, while others turned my home into a flower shop. Judy ran to get some wine to celebrate as I reported the latest news to her over the phone; June, in Boston, told me she had not received such a good phone call in years.

Moshe's doctors reacted with particular joy. His cardiologist, Dr. Zangwill, said to me, "You have made my week." His cardiac surgeon, Dr. Benson, told me, "It's like a breath of fresh air any time you call." His anesthesiologist, Dr. Davies, asserted that this was the best news I could have given him.

When I passed the news to Dr. Finkel, the neurologist who had been particularly pessimistic in his prognosis, he called it a miracle —a one-in-a-million occurrence—and added that he thought it must be due to the devoutness of the family, which must have acquired special merits "above." Both Moshe's internist and our family doctor —who had practiced medicine for forty-four years—said they had never encountered such a case. The internist thought it warranted recitation of "Praised be the author of creation"—a benediction for awe-inspiring natural phenomena.

Several friends cried openly when they saw Moshe at home. Hillel told me he had come "to see the living miracle." Shlomo said he had flown in from Boston to offer the benediction "Praised be thou, O Lord, who resurrects the dead" in Moshe's presence. Both Moshe and I broke down when he recited these deeply moving words.

Two friends, both Bible scholars, viewed Moshe's recovery from the biblical frame of reference. Nahum claimed that if Moshe's story had appeared in the Bible, it would have been considered a myth. Noel wrote, "I am totally overwhelmed by what happened. It is like a parable, and a parable of the whole Bible, which is also the story of a people who were destroyed and came back to life."

The first letters from Moshe also aroused strong emotional reactions in all who received them. They repeatedly used the words *thrill* and *joy* in response to seeing his handwriting again. Frank, well known for never answering letters, replied to Moshe's first letter, which arrived around Christmas. He called it "the most marvelous of gifts in this season of gifts"; adding, "The familiar script reduced me to tears." Moshe reacted, tongue in cheek, "One has to die in order to get Frank to write."

All kinds of stories concerning Moshe's recovery made their rounds in Jerusalem and Boston. In one fictitious tale, a nurse gave the comatose Moshe a wrong injection, as a result of which he recovered. The purpose of this story was presumably to emphasize the seemingly miraculous nature of Moshe's recovery, which could be ascribed only to a supernatural power since human powers had so obviously failed.

In another fiction about Moshe's recovery, Elisha was the hero-savior. The little fellow was supposedly brought to Moshe's bedside in the hospital and placed on top of him, whereupon Moshe awakened from his coma. In this story our grandson plays a part similar to that of the prophet whose name he bears. For did not the first Elisha revive the son of the Shunamite woman by lying on top of his lifeless body? Both stories are equally miraculous.

❖ ❖ ❖ 32 ❖ ❖ ❖
# Imminent Release

In light of Moshe's marked progress, we asked Dr. Margolis, head of the rehabilitation unit, to re-examine him. We hoped that the doctor would now agree to take Moshe into his special unit on Mount Scopus.

Only three weeks after the first examination (a month after his awakening), Moshe knew where he was. He gave the correct answer to the arithmetic problem three times twelve, and he knew the number of quarters in one whole, but he answered six times twelve and one hundred divided by twenty-five incorrectly.

"What is the name of the Prime Minister?" asked Dr. Margolis.

"Shamir."

"The name of the Defense Minister?"

"Dayan."

These two gentlemen no longer served in those roles. Dayan was two years dead. It appeared that Moshe's long-term memory was fine, but his short-term memory was not.

Moshe used the left side of his body on request—the "neglect" of that side had gone. His aphasia was improved. More and more of his automatic actions and memories were returning.

Tearfully, Moshe reported a toilet accident to Dr. Margolis—he felt humiliated about it.

Dr. Margolis believed that Moshe's depression and aggression (we had told him about the latter) were partly triggered by his hospitalization and that they might hamper his improvement. Moshe needed his privacy in order to derive the most benefit and enjoyment from his family and from familiar objects. Therefore, he concluded, to our great amazement, that *Moshe should be released from the hospital and should come home* as soon as his diabetes had been stabilized! His own home, claimed Dr. Margolis, would be the best rehabilitation unit for Moshe.

The news hit me like a bombshell. But as I let it sink in, it began to make sense. Moshe had made such headway at each home visit that it was apparent home really was the best medicine for him. But we would have to reorganize the apartment to make it safe for him to live there.

Tamara visited Yad Sarah, the medical-equipment loan society, and brought home a bedrail, handrails for support at the toilet (a week later, Moshe fell while standing alone in the washroom at the hospital), and a wheelchair. We also hired a walker. I bought handrails for the bath.

By Friday we were all set up for Moshe's first Sabbath at home. On the way out of the ward, Alon took Moshe to see Professor Kalman, a former colleague and a patient of four years' duration in the chronic geriatric ward. Moshe cried when he saw his pitiable state and exclaimed, "There but for the grace of God go I." Throughout that Sabbath Moshe recalled the encounter and repeatedly said to Alon, "You shouldn't have shown him to me. It upset me far too much."

Both Moshe and I were greatly moved when I lit the Sabbath candles. The boys wheeled him to the synagogue, about three blocks away. I walked a little behind them. When I saw people coming to welcome Moshe, I was so overcome by emotion that I ran straight home, so that I would not be seen weeping. Later, Moshe criticized one of our friends for saying only "How nice to see you" when they met in synagogue. Moshe felt the situation warranted something more.

Back at home, Moshe spoke of being "half dead." I argued: "No, you are three quarters all right." He turned this into a game: "Four fifths."

"Six sevenths."

"Eight ninths."

Our sons and their womenfolk, as well as my mother and uncle, were all present at the Friday evening dinner. Moshe made the Kiddush (ceremonial blessing over the wine) as head of the family, but he interrupted himself by bursting into tears. Everyone at the table cried with him. Moshe also made the blessing over the loaves and cut one of them unaided, so that each of us got a piece. (This too is a part of the Sabbath ceremony.)

Moshe had eaten the last few Friday evening dinners at the hospital, usually in the presence of Shraga. This time he praised my food and was angry when somebody facetiously compared it with the hospital food—he could not bear to be reminded of anything associated with the hospital.

Each of us took a turn at night duty with Moshe. Alon brought intercom equipment and showed Moshe how to press the button in case he needed someone to attend to him. Moshe kept Alon up that first night at home and was most distressed when he had an "accident." Both boys helped to clean him, but Moshe claimed that in the hospital they took better care of him. This was no doubt true since the orderlies were more experienced in this area. But Moshe's denigration of Alon's and Jonathan's ministrations was probably also a coverup for his shame.

The following day he was again wheeled to the synagogue and he cried during the reading of the Torah.

Throughout Friday and Saturday there was a stream of visitors, including Professor Patenkin, the president of Hebrew University. Moshe felt in his element and reacted appropriately to each visitor. The president asked him if he knew a certain scholar from Chicago. "Yes, I even own his book," Moshe said. He told him the exact position of the book, adding that it had a blue cover. Professor Patenkin climbed the ladder and found the book exactly where Moshe had said it was, and with a blue cover.

On Saturday afternoon Rodney spoke very carefully to Moshe about the "slight" brain damage affecting his arithmetic and sense of spatial orientation. This upset Moshe greatly. He thought it meant "everything is bad" and maintained that he had not been aware of these problems.

Later that day, Alon studied a text by Maimonides with him. Moshe read and understood the words but could not understand the broader meaning. Fortunately he was unaware that he was not up to his former competence.

At the close of the Sabbath it was Moshe who made Havdalah (the benediction over the wine) to signal the conclusion of the Sabbath.

By the end of that evening he was quite confused. It had been a very full day for him. Alon's kidding made him angry.

During the following night, when I was on duty, Moshe called out every half hour, often unaware that he was doing so. He was almost dry in the morning but wanted to get up at 4:45 A.M. I insisted that he sleep for another hour, after which Jonathan dressed him and helped him put on his phylacteries for morning prayers. Moshe was able to stand for some of these prayers.

He was happy to have been at home for a whole weekend, but he realized he would have to return to the hospital until his diabetes was under control.

When he came home for his next visit, Moshe walked up to his chair in his study with a walker. Had he moved to the right by a few inches he would have prevented colliding with the chair. Instead he turned left in a circle. Evidently he still had some left-sided neglect.

He told Jonathan that I had said he no longer needed a bedrail. Alas, this was pure wishful thinking on his part. He obviously did not want to be considered a patient any longer.

Later, we watched a comedy on television and he laughed at the jokes in an exaggerated way. After a short while, however, he ceased to show any interest in it, claiming that it was a waste of time and not good for his health. Jonathan asked him what he was doing with his time. "Actually, nothing," he replied. That decided him to start reading again—he had done very little reading so far. He was reading a book when I came to see him the following morning.

In physiotherapy he was practicing walking up and down stairs with a four-pronged cane and also doing pulley work with his arms, raising them alternately. He said: "Jesus, Maria, and Joseph" softly after each exercise, adding, "I am swearing again."

Since a group of muscles in the back of his left foot were paralyzed (this is known as a drop foot), he had to wear a brace in order to raise this foot when he walked. He used his critical faculties in this context: "I have to ask questions," he said, "not merely to receive instructions, but to see how harmful the brace is." As of now the doctors would have to treat him as an adult of sound mind. So far they had communicated to us, his family, about him.

Unfortunately Moshe's memory for recent events still left a lot to be desired. He did not remember that Jonathan and Yona had visited him the day before or even that Jonathan had been there again that very morning. He confused Yona and Tamara and therefore kept talking to Alon as if it were he who was about to marry Yona. To help Moshe, Alon tried to reason with him.

"Do I have a son?" he asked.

"Yes."

"What is he called?"

"Elisha."

"What is his mother called?"

"Tamara."

"So it couldn't be Yona, could it?"

"No."

"You see, I am already married to Tamara," Alon concluded. This kind of dialogue was repeated several times, since Moshe had trouble integrating Yona into his consciousness.

His ability with numbers remained shaky. For example, he could not calculate the amount of time between a quarter to two and two o'clock, and he thought that there was a half hour between two and three o'clock.

On the other hand, his memory of the past never ceased to amaze us. Meeting our electrician, who always boasts that he is saving us from certain death by fire, he called out to him, "Shimon, tell me that everything has been burned." In response to Jonathan's wanting him to wash his hands, he asked, "Am I Lady Macbeth?" Putting a paper tissue in his pocket, he quoted Shylock: "Put money in thy purse." Most incredible was his reaction to Adina's instruction that he stand with his "chest out." This phrase reminded him of something our dance teacher had told us thirty-two years earlier! He discussed the Shapira forgery with another patient and told him that he had written an article about it. That was also some thirty-odd years ago. So too was the fact that he had been asked to sit in on one of Bill's lectures— Bill was a new lecturer at the university at that time. Moshe recounted the incident during one of Bill's visits to him.

❖

Most amazing for those present in the synagogue that Sabbath—five weeks after his awakening—was the sight of Moshe proceeding with his walker to the lectern, where the Torah was being read, to make a blessing for the reading of the Law. The climax came when he benshed Gomel. Standing before the Torah scroll, he made the benediction of deliverance on recovering from his life-threatening illness. It had been his idea to make the benediction now rather than waiting until restored to full health, as Alon had suggested.

Mr. Brin, one of the congregants, was particularly moved on this occasion. When Moshe was still in Hadassah Hospital, he had told Alon that he had had a dream in which Moshe was called up to the Torah in synagogue and then benshed Gomel. In the dream, Moshe then turned to the congregation to thank them for their prayers on his behalf during his time of affliction. Mr. Brin had assured Alon that his dream would be fulfilled. Now, he felt certain, was the time of its fulfillment.

❖

Moshe's need for my presence increased from day to day. He could not understand why I should go home or why I needed to eat. Neither could he tolerate my talking on the phone even when Shraga or some other close friend was with him. It was clear that for him I had no function other than that of his helpmate.

I still had to be careful how I spoke to him. When I said, "Now we go to the toilet," Moshe protested, "I hate 'we' as used by Charles Laughton's nurse." (In *Witness for the Prosecution*, a film we had seen during the year preceding his operation, Laughton portrays a wheelchair-bound old lawyer). He understood very well that this usage is typical of the mothers of young children and the caretakers of very old and usually senile patients. He refused to allow me to put him into either category.

Moshe was showing more independence. He put his slippers on alone for the first time one day and tried to close a button on his pajamas the next. When he could not manage this feat he cried in frustration.

Moshe had forgotten how to use telephone tokens and asked Jonathan to instruct him about this. So far he had relied on orderlies and nurses to place calls for him from public telephones. But since he wanted to be able to call people on his own, he relearned the skill.

Alon had become used to giving his father instructions. Moshe wondered to Tamara and Jonathan whether he would ever be able to resume the role of father vis-à-vis Alon and undo the reversed father–son relationship.

Weekend nights were difficult. He used the bell frequently or not at all. Like a baby, he often cried in his sleep and whenever he woke up he was confused and did not know where the objects he needed were, although they had been placed on the night table next to his bed. On one occasion he asked for toast at midnight "as I get for breakfast at the hospital." He added, "I'm having such a good time eating." Who could begrudge him such innocent pleasures?

Often he insisted on getting up at two in the morning. Once during Jonathan's night shift, Jonathan let him get up and gave him a book to read; Moshe fell asleep in his easy chair until five.

He was angry that his sons made him wear diapers and insisted that they be taken off as soon as he woke up. With some persuasion he would go to sleep again and might even declare later that he was very happy *he* had insisted on going back to sleep!

❖

Dr. Benson expressed a wish to visit Moshe at home. We invited him and his wife to come one Saturday morning at eleven, six weeks after Moshe had regained consciousness. Since Moshe was an early riser, he was quite impatient by eleven o'clock and insisted on going for a walk with all of us, although we tried to hold him back. As he reached the front garden gate with his walker, the Bensons appeared. I invited everyone back into the house, but Moshe was determined to receive his visitors in front of the house, so we fetched chairs and a table and served refreshments in the courtyard, right next to the garbage cans! The Bensons were good sports and responded in a matter-of-fact way. Dr. Benson engaged Moshe in talk about his scholarly dictionary. Moshe willingly explained the nature of the dictionary to him. When I mentioned the Hebrew grammar that Moshe had written for his mother as a boy, Moshe volunteered his mother's age at the time as "ten years" correcting himself when I questioned this to "She was ten years older than I, she was twenty years old." Obviously there was still much room for improvement in Moshe's ability with numbers!

Moshe had not played the game according to acknowledged social rules when he refused to have Dr. Benson and his wife go into the house with him. But he acted more appropriately that afternoon when Miriam, Yona's mother, came to see him for the first time. He apologized for not getting up when she entered the room and used the correct social formula, "It was nice meeting you," at the end of her visit.

Yet Moshe was still childish at times. Seeing someone eating ice cream in the park, he insisted that he too must have some ice cream. But it was the Sabbath, and the stores were closed. Moshe would not take no for an answer. Fortunately, Alon showed some creative thinking that saved the day: he crushed a few ice cubes, poured raspberry juice over them, and thereby satisfied Moshe.

❖

Seven weeks after regaining consciousness Moshe not only dressed himself (though at times he put his pants on over his pajama bottoms) but also proudly related this fact to Bayla, while chatting with her and inquiring about her work and her husband. In the ward, he was concerned that the toilet door be properly closed behind him. He valued his privacy.

The family used every occasion that presented itself to test Moshe's knowledge of important dates. I told him that people were preparing a birthday party for him and asked him whether he knew how old he was.

"They'll find that out," he replied evasively.

"Which birthday is it?"

"The last one."

"What year were you born?"

He responded correctly: "1925."

"But what year is it now?"

"'65, no, '85."

We went back and forth in this way until Moshe tired of it and complained that I was asking him the kinds of question one asks a complete idiot.

When Jonathan visited him at the hospital that evening, Moshe insisted that he wanted to go home. Jonathan repeatedly told him that he was coming home the following day. Each time Moshe agreed, only to repeat a little while later, "So let's go." He appeared to be stuck on this idea, a sign of perseveration. As Jonathan got ready to request special permission for overnight home leave, the nurse announced a significant rise in his blood sugar, which necessitated his remaining under medical supervision at the hospital. Yona visited him an hour later. Moshe told her that he had given Jonathan a hard time—he was aware of his behavior.

At home the next day, he continued to be easily upset. He asked me for a special type of paper. I was unable to understand exactly what he had in mind and gave him the wrong type of paper. Furious about my misunderstanding, he tore the paper up.

That whole day he believed it was Friday. I had told him Barbie and David were coming over on Friday. He changed his clothes and tied his tie. It was impossible to talk him out of the Friday idea— again, he was perseverating. But that night he woke up only once— apparently being taken off all sleeping pills for three nights enabled him to sleep better. In the morning he tried to make himself a cup of coffee. Failing to find the Nescafé jar, he poured himself some apple juice instead.

During the weekend he read a whole page of the newspaper for the first time (hitherto he had read only the top half). Next he embarked on an orgy of letter-writing to friends abroad. The text of each letter was different, but all contained the following ingredients:

This is the first sign of my existence and of my return to normal functioning.
Thank you for your interest, help, and encouragement in these difficult weeks.
I am very grateful for the signs of divine grace granted to me, recalled from the brink of death.
May you be spared any such trouble.

The dates at the head of each letter were purely arbitrary. One was dated 7/12/83. (The actual date was November 23, 1985.)

Moshe started to write a speech for Chaim Rabin, a close friend and colleague, whom he planned to surprise at his seventieth birthday party.

Helping me sort through a large container of medical drugs, Moshe remembered what each one was for—diabetes, high blood pressure, cardiac symptoms—and wrote labels for the medicine chest.

❖

Twenty-two weeks after surgery, eight weeks out of his coma, Moshe complained more vehemently than ever about having to return to the hospital. "Who invented the Shaare Zedek Medical Center?" he wanted to know. He did not know how to occupy himself there in the afternoons, when no member of the family was there. Although he knew I was seeing patients, he walked to Mrs. Nathan's office and asked her to call me at home. He wanted one of our sons or me with him and told me plainly that there was no need for me to see patients. He was particularly upset if I was out when he called, especially if the boys did not know where I was.

Moshe could not read, listen to music, or watch television when he was alone. He read only when one of us was present. He became aware of the background music when I was near him—in fact, it often moved him to tears. Moshe seemed like a young child who cannot play in the absence of the mother and needs a mediator or comforting presence in order to occupy himself.

He did show consideration to those not so close to him. When a patient with whom he shared a room demanded silence in the evening, he and Yona communicated by writing each other notes in English. In one of these notes he asked her if her parents allowed her out so late in the evening and then sent her home to sleep.

He was more willing than ever to communicate with pen and paper. Thus he agreed at once when I asked him to write to my brother Gershon and his wife, Linda. Moshe wrote:

Dear Ger and Linda,

This is the first occasion that I can write to you to thank you for all your interest. Thank God I am out of hospital and only there for a weekend. [He was indulging in wishful thinking here —actually he spent weekends at home and the week in the hospital.] To inform you about the latest development—Jonathan is engaged to be married. . . . She is a lovely girl and has already shown her qualities. . . . We are totally in love with our new daughter.

The most moving letter Moshe wrote was to his cousin Ursel in Berlin, one of the very few relatives he has, six weeks after regaining consciousness. It was written on the right side of the paper and the date was a cryptic 81/1821. Times and dates seemed to have lost all significance for him. But since Moshe wrote the letter in German, his mother tongue, he gave the most honest account of events as he perceived them:

> My dear Ursel,
>   I send you today one of the first letters I have written since my illness. I know you were concerned about me during that dreadful time and first of all I want to thank you for that. Thank God I am able to write now—after all the problems with coma the whole thing looks unlikely and I am thankful many times over that these days have been given to me as a gift. . . . The doctors here had given me up and I am grateful many times that I exist and am able to write. So we will have opportunities to meet one another although I am still tied to my walker. Also, my emotional state is still terribly labile and the excitement is a part of the whole situation—but the situation just has to be accepted. You will now have a cousin who is damaged. Now you know the most important news, not exactly ideal, but that is how it is.

For this purpose Moshe looked for "Fisch" under *A* in the telephone directory, trying to find the phone number of Ursel's relatives in Tel Aviv, family Fisch, in order to check her address. He quickly became frustrated when this was unsuccessful. And his specialty is dictionaries, which are arranged in alphabetic order! Luckily he found Ursel's address in one of his address books.

At about this time he sat at his desk and went through his bank statements. He called up his bank manager, who had visited him when he was unconscious, and told him he had been abroad! When I asked why he had made up that story, Moshe replied, "Why should I say I have been in the hospital?" He was unaware that his condition had been the talk of the town.

He examined his university paycheck and the stubs of my check-books just as he had done before he became sick. He was delighted

Moshe's first letter to his cousin Ursel, written seven weeks after he
regained consciousness.

that he had continued to earn money during the weeks he had not worked. "Now Jonathan can get married," he concluded.

The time had come, Moshe believed, to talk to Yossi and Miriam about Yona's forthcoming wedding to Jonathan. We had all been upset that Moshe could not attend their engagement party and had decided to postpone the wedding until he could participate fully. We expected to wait until August.

Moshe felt he could now afford to help set up the young couple in their forthcoming married life. He made a six-point plan for his talk with Miriam and Yossi—reassuming his responsibilities as head of the family. The meeting was fixed for Channukah.

Moshe had not altogether returned to his former self, however. He complained that reading no longer gave him any pleasure. But he agreed to read Agnon, one of his favorite authors, with Yona. Moshe now explained to Yona those words and phrases that she did not understand. The old teacher was reappearing.

Moshe's demands to come home were more insistent now. After the weekend with us he phoned Alon repeatedly, telling him that he refused to stay in the hospital. Moshe said clearly that he was depressed not to be in charge of his own life; he had obviously reached the limits of endurance in the hospital. Rachel also told us that Moshe was far more alert in his work on the dictionary at home than in the ward. We decided it was high time to obtain Moshe's final release from the hospital.

❖ ❖ ❖ 33 ❖ ❖ ❖

## Homecoming

November 27, 1985—a day of great joy. Moshe was finally to be released from the hospital, a little over five months after his surgery. Rachel went to see him early that morning and packed up all his belongings. At ten she called to say that Moshe was impatiently asking where we were.

We decided to celebrate Moshe's departure from the hospital by throwing a small party for the staff of the chronic geriatric unit. (It is a rare occurrence indeed that patients leave that unit at all, let alone in such good shape.) I cried with excitement throughout the speeches by Alon and Mrs. Nathan. When I finally took leave of Mrs. Nathan, she reminded me that from the start she had held out hopes for a happy ending. But which of us had wholeheartedly believed in such a possibility when we took Moshe to that unit twelve weeks earlier?

Bringing Moshe home was like bringing home a newborn infant. He was certainly newly reborn to the world. I felt not a little apprehensive since the responsibility for his care would now fall primarily upon me. Nor would I be able to run to the nurses or doctors with every medical problem.

When a baby is collected from the hospital, the father usually accompanies the mother, sharing both the joys and the new burdens. Our sons, unasked, now took over the role of the father in helping to care for the "reborn" Moshe.

Alon, Tamara, and Elisha moved into our house so that they could help attend to Moshe twenty-four hours a day. Jonathan was still living at home.

Alon had learned how to take a blood sample from Moshe's finger to test if his blood sugar was high. We called in Rodney the first morning this was necessary. Fortunately, Moshe's subsequent urine tests showed no evidence of sugar, so we did not have to take further blood samples.

Alon, Jonathan, and I took turns at night shifts. But after a few days I told Alon and his family to return home so that they could lead a more normal life. I knew I could manage on my own with Jonathan's help. He, in turn, got regular support from Yona, of whom Moshe grew more and more fond. He said to me after talking to her one day: "I feel this girl is really entering the family."

The boys helped Moshe in and out of his bath. He needed no help getting dressed, except for putting on his shoes.

Back at home Moshe went straight to his desk but was upset when he found he could not read his own handwritten jottings. Nor could he remember any phone numbers. "My head won't cooperate," he sighed. Yet he stated his intention to go to his office in the Old City the following week.

He now made a habit of writing at his desk and began to express resentment at unexpected visitors. Why could anyone who felt like it just drop in on him merely because he was at home? I became the mediator between him and his visitors. He seemed to want to return to his old work habits and to keep business and pleasure apart.

To help Moshe regain the full use of his limbs, we asked a physiotherapist to work with him at home three times weekly. As part of his therapy, Moshe walked up and down the corridor of our apartment with a four-pronged cane. On one such occasion, Shula came to visit. When Moshe saw her, he intoned the well-known Schubert song "Das Wandern ist des Müllers Lust" (Strolling is the miller's joy) as an ironic comment on his activity.

Racheli, the director of Moshe's Israeli publishing house, had phoned several days earlier. Wishing to cheer me up, and unaware that Moshe had regained consciousness, she asked whether she could show me the proofs of the new illustrated Haggadah (the tale of the Exodus read on Passover night at the Seder) that Moshe had edited. I told her she could show them to Moshe himself. She was overjoyed to hear that he had recovered, and twenty-four hours after his return home, she brought him the proofs. Moshe had completely forgotten his involvement with this Haggadah and was delighted to see the proofs. His comments about them were absolutely pertinent.

Moshe was most delighted by Racheli's request a few days later that he prepare a preface to the Haggadah. (She had first asked me if I thought he was up to the task.) The last paragraph of the preface he ultimately wrote (translated from Hebrew) reads as follows: "I give praise and thanks to the One who rescued me from the serious illness that overtook me in those days when I was working on this edition. Praise and thanks be to Him."

Then Ezra, a friend and colleague, brought Moshe some reprints of his latest articles, which he read as soon as Ezra left. That evening I found him sitting up in bed reading the newspaper, as in the days of old. Later that week, sitting unoccupied, he criticized himself: "I should now read the newspaper. I cannot just sit here waiting." His old love of reading seemed to have returned once he was back in his usual setting. How right Dr. Margolis had been in maintaining that Moshe's best rehabilitation unit was home!

Rachel bought him a calendar and address book, and he eagerly recorded in it the addresses and phone numbers of people who were important to him.

Three days after his release from the hospital, Moshe walked up three flights of stairs, supported by Alon and Shraga, to attend Chaim Rabin's seventieth birthday party. Chaim could hardly believe his eyes and declared Moshe's visit the most beautiful birthday gift he had received. All this had been Alon's idea. When Batya, Chaim's wife, had called to invite us, I had regretfully declined on Moshe's behalf. But when I reported this to Alon, he asked, "Why shouldn't Dad go?" He suggested the idea to Moshe and even asked him whether he wanted to prepare a little speech for Chaim. Moshe's appearance and the speech he delivered—without even looking at his script—stole the show that evening.

❖

When Moshe was released from the hospital the Jerusalem health department assigned a caretaker to him three times weekly for three hours. The caretaker, specially trained to work with the handicapped and the elderly, was to help Moshe with his washing, dressing, and whatever else was required.

Moshe absolutely refused to be helped in his toilette by a strange woman and was furious when I tried to show one of the caretakers how to pull up his pants in the bathroom. I thereupon decided that the caretaker should go for walks with Moshe, enabling me to do whatever I needed to do during that time. But Moshe did not take kindly to any of these women, even though they had been trained for sensitivity and tact. He did not enjoy these walks.

On one such walk he and the caretaker went to a nearby hotel and ordered coffee. When it was time to pay, Moshe discovered that he did not have enough money with him. The waitress knew Yaffa, the caretaker, and agreed to let her bring the money later. But Moshe could not stop talking throughout the day about the shame and indignity he had experienced when he realized he had insufficient money. Nothing we said could stop his harping on this humiliating experience.

Whenever I went out and left him with a caretaker he was upset. "You left me with a strange woman," he complained. "I couldn't work because I couldn't find my papers." It seemed that I or one of the boys had to be around for Moshe to feel comfortable enough to function. He was particularly annoyed if the caretaker arrived as we were having breakfast together. This seemed an intrusion on our intimacy, and he expressed his displeasure by hissing.

A month after his return home, Moshe decided he absolutely did not want a caretaker. He said he did not wish to waste public money! The person in charge of the caretakers could not believe that we were no longer in need of a helper. She feared that these professionals had not done their work to our satisfaction.

Moshe's appetite improved greatly once he was back home. At first he took second helpings of each course, which gave him indigestion. But he quickly learned his lesson and ate only as much as agreed with him. He wanted to have the same food as everyone around him and became angry when I served him special sugarless cake. He was upset still to be considered a patient.

It was hard at first to make it clear to Moshe that he had certain difficulties with which he needed help. For example, he denied that he had problems with numbers. In fact, he told everyone that I had invented these problems. Jonathan tried to demonstrate his difficulties by asking me to solve easy problems that Moshe had claimed could be mastered only by professors of mathematics. I am notoriously weak in arithmetic. When I solved the problems correctly, Moshe had to admit that he needed help in this area. Jonathan, careful to cushion the blow to Moshe's ego, assured him that we still loved him and that he could improve through tutoring.

Moshe's orientation in time remained very poor. He thought that every day was Friday; thus he was daily preparing himself mentally for the Sabbath, which starts on Friday evening.

Moreover, he functioned at a low boiling point, tending to overreact to whatever he perceived as my interference in his life. He became very angry when he thought, wrongly, that I was trying to get him to go to bed. Also, he was extremely annoyed when I placed some reprints before him. "You are pushing them down my throat. Don't do it, please. Don't run after me," he pleaded and then shouted, in tears, "I can't live here!" He even blew up once when I offered to accompany him to the university. There was no point in arguing or trying to show him that he had misperceived or misinterpreted a situation. I just had to let things blow over, aware that Moshe was eager to prove to himself and others that he was an independent adult again.

Nights were still difficult. He screamed during the night, without being aware of it. He was often confused when he woke up. But once, realizing what a bad night he had given me, he apologized most movingly: "Poor Mummy, having such a terrible husband!"

❖

Tamara's friend Lori, a speech therapist, had just arrived from Boston. With my permission, Tamara asked her for a consultation. Lori found that Moshe could not always name common objects immediately. But when she asked him: "What falls?" he replied unhesitatingly, "A proud man who comes down." His pride must have been badly shaken by her questions.

Fortunately, Moshe was due for an ego boost. Only four days after his return home, Shraga and Moshe Bar-Asher, head of the Institute for Jewish Studies at Hebrew University and a former student of Moshe, called for him at home and brought him to the university. There Moshe received a big welcome from his assistants and colleagues as well as from the dean. He was exceedingly happy.

Moshe brought his mail home and, sitting at his desk, went through it. He also started to read a journal he had been sent.

Moshe felt it was time he started working, but he was too unsteady on his feet to obtain the required books from his bookshelves. He asked us to arrange his books within reach.

He became upset when I looked for receipts in the drawers of his desk, maintaining that I carried them in my pockets and always forgot where I put them. This was a projection, since Moshe was continually forgetting where he had put things. Frequently Shraga and Rachel were roped in to supplement our efforts to find what had been misplaced.

Jonathan made Moshe a list of where things were before he went to sleep: "Your slippers are in front of the bed," and so on. The list served as a crutch, similar to the walker he needed.

Moshe also jotted down on his calendar items that he needed to take care of. With the help of this device, his memory for recent events improved. He reminded me to call our family doctor to ask him to write a prescription; he also remembered that his assistant was coming to visit that morning.

Yet some memory problems remained. For example, Moshe would ask a friend to accompany him to the university the following morning. When the friend arrived, he frequently found that Moshe had asked another person to take him to the same place at the same time. Moshe had completely forgotten the previous arrangement, and in his anxiety about getting to the university he had made doubly sure that he would have company—or even a driver.

Furthermore, the reminders Moshe wrote in his calendar often were written on arbitrary dates—even meetings that occurred on specific dates. As a result, he rarely found the reminders he needed, just as he could not remember where he had put things.

Yet Moshe frequently amazed me with his recall of events from the past. A week before Christmas, about nine weeks after he regained consciousness, he recalled the Christmas in 1952 when he and I had first met. He wondered if I remembered walking with him through the snow of the English countryside and hearing the Queen's Christmas broadcast through the open windows.

During that week Moshe heard that *King Lear* was being shown on television. Although the play started at 10:20 P.M., he wanted to stay up and watch it. At the end he exclaimed amid tears, "What a great play!"

❖

His friend Henry, an elementary school classmate, visited from Paris. They exchanged reminiscences about their Berlin childhood. Moshe recalled the events of those years almost perfectly. His first visit with Henry in at least twelve years was most meaningful to him.

A week later Moshe made his own breakfast for the first time and even boiled water for coffee. That evening we visited Harriet and Dan. Moshe behaved suitably in the company of old friends. When we took our leave and went down to the garage, I had forgotten which direction we had to take to reach our car. But Moshe remembered! His spatial orientation had obviously improved. Mine had not!

To top it all Moshe and I attended our first concert together after his operation, at the Jerusalem Theater. Later he told Yona how much he enjoyed walking through the main entrance. He felt like a human being (*ben adam*) again. The president of the Hebrew University was delighted to see Moshe there, and asked if he might have the pleasure of accompanying him to the restroom at intermission. I could hardly decline such an offer (especially since I was not allowed into the men's room!). Moshe's friends and colleagues seemed eager to do any small service for him. Moshe himself was at the point where he did not always take kindly to being chaperoned, since he no longer considered himself to be ill. In fact, he turned the tables and extended help to others in need: when Jonathan developed back trouble, it was Moshe who helped him to dress and undress.

❖

Our friend Chaim Soloveitchik called me one day to ask how Moshe was faring.

"What does he do all day long?" he wanted to know.

"Work at his desk," I replied.

"Pardon?" he asked increduously, convinced—as he told me later —that my answer was pure wishful thinking. It was inconceivable to him that Moshe would ever again do intellectual work.

Ten weeks after coming out of the coma Moshe practiced putting one foot in front of the other while walking with his physiotherapist. He was able to walk with a simple four-pronged cane now, without additional support. When attending synagogue he no longer required a wheelchair or walker. And he now slept through the night without calling anyone, after I warned him that I would otherwise need to sleep in a different room since I desperately needed a whole night's rest. The morning after that warning, he asked me, with much feeling, if I loved him. But most important, after Rodney examined him and told him that he was in good shape, Moshe at long last really believed that he was getting better.

# ❖ ❖ ❖ 34 ❖ ❖ ❖

## Happy Channukah

It was the most memorable Channukah we ever celebrated. The Feast of Lights commemorates the miraculous historical victory of a small number of Jews over the powerful Greek army, whose soldiers had defiled the Temple. When the victorious Jews came to light the candles at the Temple, they found that there was only enough oil for one day. But the flame miraculously burned for eight days.

This Channukah we celebrated a living miracle: Moshe had been restored to us and released from the hospital twelve days previously. When he lit the Channukah candles on the first night of the festival and recited the prayer concerning "the miracles that You made for our forefathers in those days, at that time," he wept uncontrollably. There was not a dry eye in the room.

For the Channukah song "Maoz Zur" (Rock of Ages) we have a family tradition: all those present at the kindling ceremony form a human train, each individual clasping the waist of the person in front. This train wends its way slowly through the apartment, singing "Maoz Zur." As always, Moshe headed the train. The only difference was that he held onto his walker as he led the procession.

Later, as I distributed the Channukah presents I had bought for each family member, the thought crossed my mind, "I'll never get another gift from Moshe. But who cares as long as I have him back? After all, *he* is the greatest Channukah gift."

That evening Moshe asked me if there was any present I would like to have. I was thrilled and told him of some beautiful items I had seen in a certain shop.

The following day Moshe seemed to have forgotten the topic, but I savored the very fact that he had raised it at all. That afternoon, Moshe woke Jonathan from his afternoon nap and told me they were going for a walk. When they came home they reported that they had gone as far as the park—quite an undertaking for Moshe. I had no reason to disbelieve them, though I wondered why Moshe had decided to go for a second walk that day.

In the evening, after the candle-lighting, Moshe took me aside and gave me a small wrapped package. When I opened it, I found an exquisite silver necklace which he had chosen for me, with Jonathan's help, in the shop I had recommended. Enclosed was a handwritten note: "With much love and thanks for your unfailing help and love."

No present has ever moved me more. Moshe was now able to feel and express his gratitude to me and even to plan to surprise me. My heart leaped with joy.

❖

During the Channukah week Moshe went to his Bar Ilan University office in the Old City for the first time since his operation. Alon first took him in a wheelchair to the Western Wall, where both of them said the Mincha afternoon prayers. From there Alon wheeled him to the Bar Ilan office. He was welcomed at the Channukah party there as "the living Channukah miracle." This visibly moved him. With great difficulty he had climbed the many steep steps to his room. Facing reality, he decided that he would not be able to work in that office for a while on account of the numerous steps on the way to the building and inside it.

During the same week we held a little party in our home for Jonathan and Yona, with only parents, brothers, and sisters in attendance. Moshe delivered a short speech about his recovery and then acted as chairman for the other speakers.

The forthcoming wedding was now fixed for March 31, earlier than originally scheduled because of Moshe's speedy recovery. At several points during the planning session Moshe became impatient. By 1:30 A.M. he had had enough for one day, so he opened the front door, indicating that he wanted everyone to go home.

# ❖ ❖ ❖ 35 ❖ ❖ ❖
## Day Hospital

Two weeks after he came home, on December 10, Moshe was accepted as one of twenty-two patients at the day rehabilitation unit in East Talpiot Jerusalem. This relatively new unit is primarily for stroke victims. Like stroke victims, Moshe's problems were the result of brain damage, though he did not suffer from paralysis except in part of his left foot.

At his first interview with Dr. Stein, the physician in charge of the unit, Moshe was able to give the ages of his sons as well as the year in which he had immigrated to Israel (1939, when the country was still known as Palestine). He was also able to calculate correctly the number of years he had been in the country. After some thought, he remembered the subject Jonathan was studying, but he forgot one digit of our telephone number.

He told Judith, the occupational therapist, that he worked at home. Having read his case history, she found this hard to believe and looked at me for confirmation. "You don't believe me," he said to her.

But when Moshe was asked his age he guessed it to be eighty, then forty, sixty-five, and twenty-five. In the unit's dining room, there were four tables, each with four place settings. I suggested to him that he could calculate the number of patients who ate in the dining room from the number of tables and place settings at each table. He guessed eighty. To help him, I asked him what four times four is. "Twelve," he replied.

Moshe was to visit the day hospital three times a week. The first time I helped him prepare to go, he reminded me of a child catching a schoolbus. Just as a parent checks to see that his or her child has pencils, notebooks, and sandwiches, I had to make sure that Moshe had his glasses and watch. Moshe thought he had misplaced them, and we searched for quite a while until he finally discovered them in his pocket. Because of that search, I had to race him through breakfast. I parted from him at the bus with a goodbye kiss. After returning home, he got easily upset, like a tired child. That evening we made a checklist of his personal items; he knew where each of them was.

To help Moshe overcome his spatial problems, the occupational therapist worked with him on geometric shapes. He found it difficult to put together a nine-piece jigsaw puzzle. But his language skills seemed unimpaired: when he heard the "Tuba Mirum" in Mozart's *Requiem*, he recited the whole Latin text and then translated it for my benefit. When Alon studied Midrash with him, he reported that Moshe was now able to think conceptually, as he had not been able to do four weeks earlier.

❖

He regularly complained that the driver of the bus that took him to the day hospital was very late—he should be there at 7:00 A.M. I noted down the actual times at which the driver came for him. In fact he was due at around 8:00. Seeing is believing—Moshe stopped accusing the driver of being late.

Moshe had been attending the day hospital for less than two weeks when he complained that his attendance at the unit left him too little time for work. He was still unaware of his mental state. Indignantly he reported to me that Dr. Stein had written "brain damage" in his file —and claimed that this diagnosis was utterly wrong. He wanted to skip lunch at the day hospital. But the staff considered the lunch part of a package deal for rehabilitation. Incidentally, Moshe still could not find his way to the dining room in this bungalow construction, with relatively few rooms; but he denied the problem, as he tended to deny most of his difficulties. He was angry at me for telling the nurse that he tried not to use his left hand when eating and asked me why I had to meddle in his life. He maintained that he had no trouble with numbers and accused me of making it up. He admitted that he had difficulties reproducing shapes, but he considered this an "impossible task." He realized that he used to think every day was Friday or the Sabbath, but pointed out that this problem had now disappeared.

Moshe's spatial orientation continued to improve. Judith, the occupational therapist, was very pleased that he could find his way around the unit after a month. He could even draw a map of the building. However, he still found the Wechsler Block Design test, in which a geometric figure has to be taken apart and then put back together again, extremely difficult.

Twelve weeks out of his coma, Moshe was able to look up numbers in the telephone directory—he now remembered the alphabetic sequence. He had also managed to memorize our phone number, his age, my birthday, and the birthdates of our children. Moshe often showed concern for me now, rather than remaining absorbed in himself. When I went to a concert, he asked me twice whether I was sure I had the ticket. He wished me an enjoyable time and wondered whether I would take a cab to the concert hall. It seemed like the good old days when he was concerned about my well-being and would do anything for me.

❖

I had to learn to readjust to Moshe. On the one hand I was serving him hand and foot, rushing to him whenever he called with some request. On the other, I wanted to foster his independence and to make him feel like a responsible adult again. I began by automatically writing out and signing all the checks for him. But he protested a month and a half out of the hospital, "I can do that alone." I also learned not to open his letters, as I had done during his coma. I gave him a key to the apartment and money when he went out. I let him pay for our taxis and for movie tickets. After only a few weeks, he was ordering his own taxis and being driven, unattended by any of us, to the university.

We had begun to invite friends over to dinner on Friday evenings. For five weeks, since Moshe came home from the hospital, only Alon's family, Jonathan and Yona, or my uncle Werner had come to dinner. Moshe was quieter with his friends than he used to be, but he took part in the conversation now and again.

December 24 was exactly six months since Moshe's coronary bypass. June 24 had become a red-letter day for me. I reckoned everything as taking place either before or after this date and frequently forgot other anniversaries that did not fall on the twenty-fourth of the month. What a nightmarish half year it had been! But now at last we were seeing light at the end of the tunnel.

Moshe wrote in German to Ursel in Berlin: "We are under the influence of the miracle. If one doesn't believe in God now, when will one do so? I am back to work and can't believe it myself. God's loving kindness!"

On the other hand, he had become overly sensitive and was easily hurt. Now when I teased him as I used to with "Silly you," he retorted, "I am not silly, but handicapped."

Moshe had lost sixty-six pounds during his coma, a good deal of it due to the atrophy of his muscles. None of his suits fit him. As an emergency measure he used suspenders to hold up his trousers, but this was no permanent solution, since it made him look like a beggar wearing hand-me-downs.

After several tailors had refused to alter Moshe's suits, suggesting instead that they make him new ones, my uncle finally sent his tailor to us. He had come to Israel from Vienna before World War II, and we called him our *Hofschneider* (court tailor). It seemed as if he would find lifelong work in Moshe. As a result of this man's skill, Moshe looked really good without his superfluous inches, in clothes that at last fit him. Relieved that yet another obstacle had been overcome, I said to Moshe, "We are a further step closer to normality." But Moshe hated me to talk about this, probably because it emphasized his former illness.

❖

Seven weeks after Moshe's release from the hospital, we had no visitors at all for Friday dinner. Moshe heaved a sigh of relief. Now at least he could study and read. How different from the days in the chronic geriatric ward, when he did not know what to do with himself when he had no visitors!

During the same week Moshe got up one morning at 4:00 A.M., ate breakfast, and decided to go to the university at 5:30. Instead, he took another sleeping pill, undressed, and went back to bed. When he woke up at 8:00 he walked unsteadily from the effects of the pill and would have fallen had I not caught him at the last minute. Moshe frequently took an additional sleeping pill during the early part of the morning, and he tended to drop off at odd hours of the day—once during a Sabbath lunch he could not be awakened. Yet on other days he got up at 4:00 A.M. and went to the library or the university at 6:00.

One Sabbath, two months after Moshe had returned home, there was no one to accompany him to synagogue (since none of our children was staying with us and I do not usually go). Moshe therefore planned to stay at home. But at 7:30, half an hour before the service began, he went out, locking the door behind him. He maintained that it took him thirty minutes to walk the two blocks to the synagogue (although when I took the walk with him on a later occasion, he completed it in ten minutes). "I did it though I had to force myself, but I thought otherwise I'd be tied to the house on Sabbath," he explained to me.

❖

At home and in the day hospital Moshe was practicing multiplication regularly, realizing at last that he lacked full mastery of the skill. The degree of his arithmetic disability was brought home to me when, asked to multiply a number by 80, he first multiplied it by 100, then by 20, and subtracted the second answer from the first.

Thanks to the devoted work of Barbara, the physiotherapist, he was now ready to go to the day hospital with a simple cane instead of a four-pronged one. We at home witnessed his greater daring as he stepped into his bath unaided. (I remained in the bathroom to make sure that everything was proceeding smoothly.) He refused compliments—for this accomplishment. In fact, he felt that I was making fun of him by praising him for carrying out an activity that any child could perform.

The evaluation of time was still problematic for him. One day he called me at close to two from the university to tell me he would be home at around one. He thought Purim (the carnival festival) was three weeks rather than three months away. And he frequently confused the week in which a certain lecture was to be given.

Moshe still tended to explode with the least provocation. One evening I suggested that he should have a bath at a time when Yona was in the house. He became furious at me. But fifteen minutes later he explained: "That's the leftover of my illness." Another time he vented his fury on me for ten minutes when I asked him if he had shaved. Once he cooled down, he announced that he must decide on such matters now that he was no longer ill. On a different occasion he said that since he was now dependent on other people, he might lose his temper if he had to ask for something many times. He was gaining insight into the nature of his outbursts, but he was not yet able to control them.

Moshe attended the research institute of Targum scholars whom he had convened from all over the world before he became ill. He became extremely angry when I asked whether he had participated actively. "You never asked me those things before my illness," he complained. He was quite right. I was intruding because I was anxious about his recovery, and he resented it. As a matter of fact, his trusted assistants informed me that less than three and a half months out of coma he was his old self at the Targum meetings, completely mastering material and participating fully.

❖

Moshe's letter to Edward, a friend and colleague at Oxford, gave me insight into how he felt about his present situation. "Work's back to its normal pace," he wrote. "I am working to keep up. Apart from writing this longhand [rather than typing it] things are working out alright." It was clear that his work was once again his main concern. No wonder he perseverated on that word.

❖

I had the feeling that external events, such as the death of an acquaintance or even Elisha's fever, did not touch Moshe deeply. He was still preoccupied with himself, his health, and his work. The first time he visited Yona's parents—something he had requested to do—he talked at length about his own parents and his immigration to Israel, rather than asking them about themselves.

Moshe often suffered little motor setbacks. He fell when he went to the toilet at the home of Jonathan's future parents-in-law. The following day he fell against the wall while trying to turn around. On the other hand, he went to the bus by himself. He did not want people to point out that he was making progress, but he revealed to us that he said "Thank you" to God all day long.

There were many demonstrations of Moshe's returning resourcefulness. We invited our friends Joyce and Harold for Friday dinner, but they did not know where our home was. Moshe called my uncle, who was also coming that evening, and asked him to accompany them from the synagogue.

Moshe knew what he wanted. For instance, he loves chocolate eclairs but was not allowed to have them because of their sugar content. He told Jonathan about his special wish. Jonathan called our pastry shop and asked the owner to bake him a sugarless batch. The owner, delighted to know that Moshe had recovered, was only too pleased to do him this favor.

Moshe was sensitive to any mention of his present or past state. He particularly did not want to hear any reference to the hospital. When a colleague confused Jonathan and Alon, Moshe remarked, "If that had been me, people would say I was still disoriented." When I spilled some soup, he asked what I would have said if he had done it. He obviously realized that he was being constantly and anxiously monitored.

He became very upset when he realized how much time his illness had cost him. "Why do I work so hard?" he asked rhetorically. He seemed unaware that few people had believed he would ever resume his work. What got him really angry was people's asking him how he was spending his time and whether he was already "working a little."

In a letter to my mother, Moshe expressed a lot of his feelings about his illness and hospitalization:

> The terrible time in Shaare Zedek is pushed into oblivion. We do not talk any more about my having recovered and having been locked up among the madmen of that ward. I do not know what were the sins that got me into such a state and by what merit [I deserved] the miracle that got me out. Nothing but divine will and grace. The only leftover is the weakness in the left foot and my vocal cords. That is the [whole] price I have to pay—thank God for that.

Clearly Moshe showed awareness only of his physical defects, which to us were relatively minor matters considering the brain trauma he had suffered. Nor did he mention all of his physical problems to my mother—he did not inform her about his constantly inflamed eyes. Dr. Zelig, of the Shaare Zedek opthalmology department and a member of our synagogue, took a culture to find the bacteria responsible for Moshe's eye infection. However, since Moshe had been taking large amounts of antibiotics, the culture showed nothing. When the antibiotic ointment he prescribed did not have the required effect, Dr. Zelig insisted on visiting Moshe to look at his eyes once more and to have him try out another ointment. This devoted doctor visited Moshe at home twice before the problem was eliminated.

❖

After attending the day hospital for two months, Moshe complained more than ever about the "idiotic tasks" he was set to do there— all of them, so he claimed, with built-in errors, so that they could not be solved. While his complaints had some truth to them, at their root was the bigger problem that Moshe did not realize he had mental difficulties. I would enumerate some of these difficulties saying, for instance, "I want you to learn about the new coins." He would counter, "Half the country doesn't know about the new coins." The staff and I met with Moshe to try to convince him that he still had problems, especially with numbers, with which he could be helped. But whenever Moshe felt under attack, he lashed out at me. I realized that pointing out these deficits was such a narcissistic blow to him that he had to defend himself by fighting back.

Judith suggested that Moshe lecture on one of his subjects, versions of the Bible, to other patients and staff at the day hospital. She thereby verified that he had not lost his grip on the presentation of these facts. Afterward Moshe was complimented by one and all, but this left him unimpressed. He saw the whole exercise as a test of how far he could project his voice, since his left vocal cords had been paralyzed. He knew that he was a good lecturer and did not require a lay audience to confirm it.

❖

Moshe began to take a more active interest in the movies about two months after his return home. Before his illness, he would agree to see a film only after asking me several times whether I was sure it was good, and he never went to the movies more than once a week. If the film did not live up to his high expectations, he would be upset about the wasted evening and even more careful the next time a movie was under consideration.

Now he came to me to ask what films (plural) I was planning to see during the week. He was even ready to try the Cinemateque, the film archives, which are beautifully situated in a scenic spot of Jerusalem.

However, one cannot drive a car directly to the building, which is located in a valley. One has to descend many steps in order to reach it (and of course on the way out one has to ascend these same steps). But Moshe was undaunted by this prospect. He enjoyed the movie and handled the steps well with alternating feet.

Several weeks later Moshe and I took a bus trip for the first time in order to go to the cinema (which had become a real incentive for trying out new ventures). By the time of the Israel Festival, during the first two weeks of June, Moshe went with me almost daily, sometimes even twice a day, to some cultural function—a film, a play, or a concert—and enjoyed it. But his critiques tended to be absolute, in black-and-white terms. There was no "Yes—but."

About two and a half months after regaining consciousness, Moshe and Shraga attended the eightieth birthday celebration of Professor Polotzky, Moshe's revered teacher. The professor's erstwhile students and colleagues gave lectures in his honor. Moshe was overjoyed at his reception by all present, but especially because Professor Polotzky sat next to him between lectures and told him how he had constantly inquired about him during his coma. Back at home, Moshe went to his desk to write a newspaper column for *Ha'aretz* about Professor Polotzky's contribution to the field of linguistics. He cried with excitement when the tribute was published. It was the first article he had written and published after his coma. I sent it to all his close friends, for whom it served as proof that Moshe had fully returned to the world of the living.

❖

Moshe's secretary at Bar Ilan, Esti, of whom he was particularly fond and who had visited him several times in the hospital, invited him to her wedding. He accepted Shraga's invitation to drive him there—the ride was about ninety minutes each way—and chose by himself the blazer he wanted to wear on the occasion. Everyone at the wedding was delighted to hear him make one of the benedictions in the presence of the newlyweds and to see him dance the tango with the bride. He enjoyed both the dance and the dinner, where he helped himself to several forbidden pastries. He was particularly pleased when Esti, a few weeks later, brought him photographs of himself participating in this joyful event.

Ten weeks out of the hospital, Moshe played host at home to three of the Targum scholars whom he had invited to Jerusalem from abroad. He was almost his old self as he sat at the head of the dinner table and conversed with them, merely a little quieter and less outgoing than he had been formerly.

My uncle Werner was ill at home with a cold, and Moshe suggested that we visit him. Since it was the Sabbath, we had to walk instead of driving. The trip, which used to take Moshe five minutes, now took twenty-five. But he was rewarded with regal honors—my uncle could not have been more pleased when he opened the door and found Moshe standing there.

Moshe knew that I was writing a book about his recovery from the coma. Each of us had told him about some of the events linked to this, almost by way of free association. But he had never heard the story in one piece, from beginning to end. He did not want to read what I was writing until almost two and a half months after his release from the hospital. Then he requested "the book." He asked if I would mind his writing comments in the margin. "On the contrary," I assured him, "I would welcome them."

As I watched him turn the pages, my heart felt for him; he was crying ceaselessly. Finally, as he handed back my composition, he said: "This was too moving for me. I can't comment on it." For the first time he had become aware of what had happened to him, by reading one continuous narrative.

❖

Moshe came home beaming from the day hospital, which he had been attending for two and a half months. He had been told that he need attend only once a week. His occupational therapist, he reported, had said she had nothing more to teach him. I found this hard to believe. I contacted her the following day, only to be told that Moshe did not seem to realize that he still needed therapy. Moshe now insisted that he had informed me he would *continue* to see the occupational therapist.

A major inducement for him to continue to attend the rehabilitation unit was his desire to learn to dance without a cane, so that he could dance with Yona on her wedding day. It is true that he had hopped along with his cane to the rhythm of the tango when Esti was the bride, but he wanted to do better where his daughter-in-law was concerned.

One large problem remained that kept Moshe dependent on others —he was still unable to drive a car. The orthopedic surgeon felt that Moshe would be able to drive an automatic transmission car—in which he would not need to use his partially paralyzed left foot. But the occupational therapist advised against this because she believed Moshe was not always alert. When he traveled with her by bus, he did not look out the window and sometimes tried to get off at the wrong stop.

But Moshe made inquiries and located a driving teacher for handicapped people. He told the teacher only about his injured foot, not mentioning his mental problems.

Moshe had been a seasoned driver of several decades' standing without a single accident to his record. No wonder that he was upset when Tamara waxed enthusiastic about his ability to drive when accompanied by his teacher (actually Moshe was driving too fast). I was reminded of how hurt he had felt when I had praised him for using the toilet. What an indignity!

For the first time since his surgery, three months after awakening from the coma, Moshe was contemplating travel abroad again. He had always loved to travel to foreign lands, meet new people, and see new places. To Rodney he had confided his belief that he would never again be able to travel. After all, how could he manage the airports and everything else entailed in flying from country to country? Rodney had reassured him that he would feel differently in a year's time. Little could he have guessed that only a month after this talk, Moshe had regained sufficient confidence in his physical and mental abilities to think not only of visiting faraway places but even of spending a sabbatical year abroad.

Since Moshe's resistance to attending the day hospital grew from week to week, the staff finally decided that it was pointless to force him to attend against his will. I felt sorry when they ended their contact with him after three and a half months, because I was sure that he could have profited in many ways from weekly work at the rehabilitation unit. But Jonathan's wedding was fast approaching and his thoughts were concentrated on this great event. He felt he needed the rest of his time for his work.

❖ ❖ ❖ 36 ❖ ❖ ❖
## Wedding

Relatives and friends gathered from the four corners of the earth for the double celebration of Jonathan's wedding and Moshe's miraculous revival. The London branch of the family was represented by my mother, my sister Rita, and my brother Leo. My brother Gershon brought his whole family from Los Angeles. Our dear friend Marvin flew in from Boston for the great event, as did Danny, Jonathan's close friend from New York. Marvin felt amply rewarded when he saw Moshe, who had come to welcome him with Alon at Lydda Airport.

The people closest to us came to our synagogue on the Sabbath before the wedding, when Jonathan was called up for the reading of the Law. Yona was not present since it is customary in our circles for the bride and groom not to see each other during the week preceding the wedding. The synagogue service was followed by a small reception (Kiddush) in our home. The speeches referred to Moshe no less than to Jonathan. No one was happier than Jonathan to have his father present during these eventful days.

More speeches followed at the luncheon in the neighboring hotel. Moshe was an able chairman, introducing each speaker with his old charm. He himself also held forth on this occasion, showering the couple with his blessings.

All these small celebrations served as the introduction to the great day itself, on the following Monday. When I switched on the radio that morning, I heard one of my favorite Schubert songs: "Lachen und Weinen" (Laughter and tears). There could have been no more fitting signature song for me that day.

During the ceremony, the bride and bridegroom, their parents, and the rabbi stood under a wedding canopy on the large hotel balcony. It was a rainy day, but the sun shone during the half hour of the marriage ceremony. I laughed and cried simultaneously, especially when I saw Moshe walking with Jonathan toward the marriage canopy, and when Moshe stood next to me while Jonathan slipped the ring on Yona's finger. No bridegroom deserved to be happier, for he, like Alon, had poured his very being into his father in order to bring Moshe back to us.

It is the custom among observant Jews that men and women dance in two separate circles. The bride and groom dance separately at first until they finally join up. On this occasion two additional dances involved people of the opposite sex: the bride and her father-in-law, and the father-in-law and his wife. Moshe had done his work at the rehabilitation unit—he was steady on his feet and had mastered the steps. Nevertheless, at one point during his dance with Yona he exclaimed, "We are not keeping time!"

Dr. Benson, who had not seen Moshe for three months, put in a brief appearance at the wedding. He was most enthusiastic about how much weight and muscle Moshe had gained during these months. In fact, the shirt I had bought for this occasion no longer fit him.

We had taken a hotel room so that Moshe could rest if he so desired. But he preferred to remain in the hall, enjoying the music and dancing. He did not want to miss even a moment's fun.

Later, at the wedding dinner, he held the guests spellbound with a twenty-minute speech relating the weekly Portion from the Bible, which had been read on the preceding Sabbath, to the newlyweds. He seemed (perhaps unconsciously) to want to restore himself to his former standing by announcing to all those present that he had lost none of his previous intellectual capacities.

❖ ❖ ❖ 37 ❖ ❖ ❖
# Further Improvements

My sister-in-law Linda, who arrived from Los Angeles ten days before Jonathan's wedding, stayed in a hotel with a swimming pool. She invited Moshe to take a swim, and he gladly accepted. She walked with him down the stairs of the pool, steadying him on one side, and supported him as he swam breast-stroke. He had the mistaken feeling that his left leg was sinking.

After Linda's return home I accompanied Moshe into the pool. With the aid of a life belt, Moshe did not need to be supported in the water, but he felt safer when I was near him. At long last, I also took up swimming again.

Nava, the daughter of our friends Aliza and Zvi, had a master's degree in sports education for the handicapped. At my request she observed Moshe in the pool, and for six weeks or so she volunteered to monitor his swim once a week and to teach him techniques to help him keep afloat. He could have had no more dedicated instructor.

Almost at the same time Moshe started taking Elisha onto his lap and playing with him. His face dissolved into one big smile as he looked into Elisha's eyes. The little fellow had released a whole well of feelings within Moshe which until then had lain dormant. Elisha was not critical or oversolicitous of his grandfather. Moreover, Moshe could feel superior to him physically. A special kind of loving communication developed between them. Their spirits were perfectly aligned. "Baba" (*Saba* is the Hebrew term for grandfather) became one of Elisha's favorite people. Moshe was absorbed by a feeling that seemed to change him profoundly from within. Here was the perfect balance for his compulsion to complete his intellectual labors. As the laughter and babbling went to and fro between them, I realized that Elisha was the perfect healer of Moshe's soul.

❖

At this point, Moshe decided to take up his work on Jewish biblical theology again. This was a book for which he had collected material throughout many years; he had already written several chapters. In the past, he had been disturbed by the lack of interest among Jewish scholars throughout the ages in producing such a work. He felt that they had taken over Christian theology rather than offer an alternative to people of the Jewish faith. But completing his book required the ability to conceptualize, which he had lacked for many weeks after recovering from his coma. I had doubted that he would ever regain this high-order cognitive capacity. I should have known better.

Moshe now spent every free hour working on this book. He explained this effort in one of his letters: "I am always overworking, for, having gone through these terrible months, I am always afraid of a repeat performance." It sounded logical; however, his doctor assured him that he was in better health than ever before and had nothing to fear on that account.

❖

At times I felt like Atlas, who, as I recalled from the famous Schubert song, complained: "Ich bin der unglücksel'g Atlas, Die ganze Welt muss ich tragen" (I am the unfortunate Atlas, the whole world I have to carry). All decisions and responsibilities concerning Moshe seemed to devolve on me. My children were prepared to help whenever needed, but I could not continue to encroach on their lives. After all, it is far from easy to build up a marriage, earn a living, and complete one's studies—especially in Israel.* They had given lavishly of their time and energy during the long and arduous months of Moshe's hospitalization and early rehabilitation. It was time that they lived their own lives unimpeded once again. For this reason I was resolved to call upon them only in a real emergency. That resolution, when carried out successfully, had the bonus of making me feel capable and competent.

I slipped up on occasion. Thus, one evening I heard the sound of water in the garden. Someone had watered the lawn but had forgotten

---

*Since Israeli students complete at least three years of army service before they start studying, they are often already married and may even have children when they enter the university. Most also have to earn a living at the same time. Moreover, male students have reserve duty one to two months every year (female students are exempt from reserve duty if they are married and/or twenty-five or older). So, all in all, Israeli students have a harder life than students in Western countries.

to turn off the sprinklers. Loath to waste so much water, I searched for the sprinklers outside in the dark but could not find them. Panic-stricken, I called Yona and Jonathan and asked one of them to come without delay. Jonathan appeared ten minutes later.

Moshe suggested that I join him on a short vacation inside Israel after Jonathan's wedding. When I agreed, he asked me where I would like to go and what dates would suit me, then made the hotel booking, just as in the old days! We had taken our last short trip together more than ten months ago, and in the intervening period vacations had not exactly been uppermost in my mind. Now I was not certain whether this vacation would be a strain or a relaxation, since I did not know how Moshe would feel and behave away from his home base. But since he had taken the initiative, I was willing to take the risk.

Two weeks after Jonathan's wedding, we went to Herzliah-on-sea, staying at a large hotel where we had often been in former years. Moshe found his way around the hotel completely unaided, going to the breakfast room early in the morning and from there to the garden on his own. He even swam in the warm indoor pool without my supervision—I merely had to help him in and out of the water.

Three weeks after this short vacation Moshe started to play with the idea of going on a Swiss holiday in September, after the conclusion of the Old Testament Congress, which was to take place in Jerusalem in August. He made inquiries about the air travel and places we might visit together. When he got an invitation to a congress on lexicography in Zurich, which began on September 9, that decided the issue for him: he would participate at that congress and travel with me through Switzerland afterward. He confided that he envied those who could travel without thinking about it twice. But immediately he added self-critically, "That's selfish and both un-Jewish and un-Christian. Such is life for those who are stricken."

Moshe was able to walk alone to his dermatologist, about ten minutes away. He also went unaccompanied to the bank to query the bank statements he had checked.

❖

It was ten months after Moshe's bypass surgery and five months since he had come home again. He was walking without a cane inside the house and on the university campus. And with me at his side and a cane in his hand, he went for hour-long walks in the neighborhood. He admitted envying anyone who walked normally without a cane.

He was now able to get in and out of his bath alone and called out exultantly to me one day, "I am very happy: today is the first time I managed all by myself, without you even standing by."

Moshe was taking an active part in his weekly Targum seminars. One of the participants assured me that Moshe had regained his former capacity to elevate himself above the particulars by conceptualizing and generalizing; he was able to see the forest and not merely individual trees.

He was working harder than ever on his projects and completing books he had started before his operation. I thought of him as the goose that lays golden eggs for his publisher. Moshe himself was struck by his incessant work. He wrote very fast, not bothering to correct his spelling mistakes. In a letter to his friend and colleague Noel, he wrote, "I am astonished myself at the amount of work [I am doing]. Hopefully it's not just quantity. In fact, I am frightened by the speed [with which] things are moving. I always think it won't end well. Did God spare me to laugh at me?"

Apropos of God, Moshe asked Alon one day: "When will you finish your doctorate?"

Alon replied, "Trust God."

But Moshe said, "We have exploited Him enough already."

It was Passover and Moshe unhesitatingly led the Seder, as in former days. He was surrounded by his sons and their wives, his grandson, my mother, my uncle, and me. His voice was still weak, so he did not want anyone else to join in the recitation of the Haggadah. Usually the Seder is a time for asking and arguing about the events in those faraway days. Now, when Jonathan asked a question, Moshe put him down: "You should have read up on it last night." Apparently, he wanted everything to go his own way. In fact, he himself posed interesting questions and debated the participants' responses.

People still frequently had to make allowances for him. During a dinner to which friends had been invited, he sometimes sat without talking to anyone. When he felt that he had had enough, he would start singing the Shir Hama'alot, which ushers in the grace after meals.

Everyone realized that the usual norms of behavior did not always apply to him. But there were more and more occasions when Moshe was alert and talked to visitors, of whom there were many during the Passover week.

Moshe still got upset with me, especially when he suspected that I was infringing on his autonomy. At such times he overreacted, but at least the storm passed quickly. On one such occasion, Alon asked him to be kinder to me and enumerated some of the things I was doing for him, of which he was quite unaware.

"You aren't quite yourself yet," Alon said, as if to excuse Moshe's behavior.

"Thou stickst a dagger in me." Moshe replied. He could not bear to be regarded as changed or as different from others. When I told him that Moshe Davies, his friend and colleague, wanted to see him, he shot back, "I am no longer someone to be seen."

❖

Moshe's number problem persisted, although he tended to make light of it. He confused the dates of his appointments, thinking they were a day or a week earlier, and he continually misplaced objects like pens and important papers.

❖

"Why are you being so dumb?" I muttered under my breath when he faltered. "God endowed you with so many gray cells. What prevents you from using them?" Such thoughts made me feel like a bitch, of course, and I was consumed by guilt.

I occasionally fell into another very dangerous trap, in which I discounted what Moshe said, agreeing with him but not really listening, as if he were a child. Fortunately I became aware of my behavior after a short while. Moshe's own reactions to normal problems helped break me of the habit, since they were often right on target, far better in fact than those I could have come up with myself. So I learned to give him more credit and to entrust him with various transactions of daily living.

Frequently I found myself urging Moshe, "Hurry up and get a move on!" Why had I not been endowed with more patience? I could have done with more of the milk of human kindness too. It was really hard for me to see Moshe move so slowly and to hear him constantly pleading "langsam" (slowly). He had once been a whirlwind and had often managed to juggle at least five activities at once—to the envy of those around him. Now he needed all his concentration in order to perform just one activity adequately. Was this slowing down an overcorrection, a recalibration by the Lord above?

Often it would have been far easier for me to take care of a task myself, but I realized that this was how Moshe's mother had behaved toward his father. She had done everything at top speed and as well as possible. Finally, Moshe's father had allowed her to take over for him entirely. That was not my intention with Moshe. So I forced myself to let him do slowly whatever needed to be done, even in some cases when he expected me to do it for him. I was rewarded—he improved through practice.

Happily Moshe's brain damage did not result in inertia, whose victims not only fail to initiate activities but are unable to carry them through to completion. He was not one of those unfortunates who spend long hours watching television or sitting idly in a chair. Quite the contrary!

The gist of my problem was that Moshe had made such tremendous progress over the months that I now expected him to be exactly the same as before the operation. Needless to say, this expectation was totally unrealistic. This meant that I needed to accommodate myself to a changed man while Moshe had to reaccommodate himself to life in its entirety.

However hard it was for him, it was probably not much easier for me, at least emotionally. I had to remind myself repeatedly to stop seeing and judging him as I imagined strangers were doing. He deserved his own standards and criteria.

❖

I felt it was the right time to call in Dr. Margolis, the specialist in rehabilitative medicine who had seen Moshe twice before recommending his release from Shaare Zedek Medical Center. I needed to know whether there were any specific ways in which I could further Moshe's progress.

Dr. Margolis thought that Moshe was in fine shape except for some minor matters (he used the Yiddish word *shmontses*). His left foot lacked deep sensation and a position sense, which could lead to instability when walking, since he was not always certain whether he had put his foot down. The doctor recommended that Moshe use a support, such as a cane or a wall, to keep from falling. Dr. Margolis also noticed that Moshe reacted more slowly with his left hand than with his right, but felt that he could nevertheless use an electric typewriter.

Moshe openly expressed his fear that the calamity that had befallen him once might happen again. Dr. Margolis assured him that the likelihood of this happening was no higher for Moshe than for the rest of the population.

A little over a month before the anniversary of his bypass surgery, Moshe addressed an audience of about fifty people at the Institute for Jewish Studies. He welcomed the new head of the institute and bade farewell to the two previous heads, both of whom had been his students. The problem about projecting his voice was easily solved by means of a microphone.

Two days later, he went to his office in the Old City, walking from the parking lot. He discussed with Racheli, his publisher, the publication of the first volume of his Hebrew dictionary, a collection of the language column he had published for ten years in *Ha'aretz*, and the third volume of his Arab–Hebrew dictionary. As if all this were not enough, he paid a visit to Yona's parents in the Old City.

The following day, he came before the medical committee which was to decide whether he was fit to drive a car again. His concentration was good: he could remember seven digits when recited forward and five digits when recited backward. He was also able to copy a design, so he was permitted to take his driving test.

Alon drove Moshe to Bar Ilan University (he had not been to the Ramat Gan campus since his hospitalization). On the way there, as in earlier days, Moshe gave Alon instructions on how to find his way through Tel Aviv and vicinity.

A few days later Moshe went to the dentist unaccompanied. From there he took the bus to the university, having first crossed a main street, full of traffic. Our friend Joyce happened to be sitting on the bus when she saw someone waiting at the bus stop who looked like Moshe. She dismissed the idea from her mind, believing it to be impossible, until she saw Moshe get on the bus with his four-pronged cane. She was so excited that she called me when she got home and told me it had made her day.

That same week Moshe went to Chanan, the barber, by himself. Chanan had cut Moshe's hair at Hadassah Hospital when he was still in a coma. He did not imagine then that Moshe would ever come to his shop again.

Ursel, Moshe's cousin from Berlin, came to see him three weeks before the anniversary of his surgery. Moshe was in great form and did not even cry when they hugged. By his own account, he was less labile now. I enjoyed seeing him behave in an outgoing and sociable manner, willing to listen to and answer all her questions. It was heart-warming to observe them together. She really brought out the best in him.

The English department of the Hebrew University had set up its own Institute for Advanced Studies. One of its most honored visiting participants, Professor Jacques Derrida, had agreed to discuss certain texts of the book of Jeremiah in the light of his own theories. In early June, Moshe was invited to participate in the lecture by Professor Sanford Budick, the head of the institute. He had never heard of Derrida, but I persuaded him to come along after telling him a little about Derrida's literary theory.

That evening, after Derrida had commented on the chapter under discussion, Moshe spoke for several minutes on why he believed Derrida's reading of the text to be unacceptable. He made his points cogently and with humor. People later congratulated me on his performance. But the high point came when Derrida approached Moshe at the end of the session and asked to talk to him at greater length. To me this signified that Moshe had made a true comeback to academic life. Derrida related to him as to any other scholar, without the slightest awareness of what Moshe had gone through in the previous months. Moshe, in turn, did not realize how he had been singled out by one of the most controversial literary theorists in the world.

❖

For at least half a year after Moshe's recovery from the coma, he was plagued by the inability to sleep for more than three or four hours at night. As a result, his frustration tolerance was often very low, and he was frequently so tired that he either dropped off to sleep in the middle of something he was doing or seemed only half awake and was unable to concentrate fully. He alternated taking two sedatives, nitrazepam and flunitrazepam, but they only helped him fall asleep, not to remain asleep.

Moshe complained of his sleeplessness to anyone who would listen, but to no avail. The doctors maintained that at his age four hours of sleep at night were enough and suggested that he nap during the day.

After six months of this misery, Dr. Aron, my mother's London physician (who had sent the comatose Moshe the "miracle drug"), made another indirect appearance. It happened that my mother had suffered for years from sleeplessness until Dr. Aron had prescribed a tranquilizer, promethazine hydrochloride, to be taken together with a sedative, prothiazine, each night. That solved her sleeping problems once and for all. When she told Dr. Aron about Moshe's sleeplessness, he suggested the same medication. Moshe's physician agreed with the prescription. The success was instant: from this time on he slept until at least seven every morning and felt refreshed when he got up. He was now able to eat breakfast with me in the mornings. He was extremely happy to be relieved of this stubborn symptom.

Trouble arose when we went on a vacation to Netanya, on the coast of Israel, and Moshe left the pills at home. I had to phone all the pharmacists in town to ask whether they had these drugs and whether they could sell them to Moshe without a prescription. After much effort, I managed to locate a pharmacist who was prepared to let Moshe have one pill so that he could look forward to at least a few hours of sleep during his vacation.

❖

About five months after Moshe regained consciousness Alon pointed out to him that flying off the handle at the slightest provocation can be tolerated only in young children or patients. To which category did he want to be assigned? Moshe chose not to be categorized in this way. With that choice his tantrums disappeared.

When Moshe was aggressive toward me in the chronic geriatric ward, I was able to dissociate myself from the pain by seeing him as a patient rather than as my husband. Gradually my perception of him changed. Proof of this was given when I cried for the first time in reaction to his saying something hurtful to me. I realized then that the insulation I had developed by serving as Moshe's therapist was wearing off. I was on the way to becoming his wife again.

❖ ❖ ❖ 38 ❖ ❖ ❖

# Epilogue

## A Different Moshe

It cannot be denied: Moshe is not the same person he used to be. There is a touching, gentle quality to him now because he is so vulnerable. He is more passive; he tends to react to talk rather than initiate it. He is more dependent on family members—he needs to speak to his children, at least by telephone, often several times daily. At the same time, he has striven to be his own master since recovering consciousness. He tried to take over money matters a short time after returning home. He phones the doctors he needs, the assistants who work with him, and his publisher when he has a question concerning one of his books.

Food and especially sleep are vital in determining Moshe's well-being and mood. When he is satiated and rested he is less easily frustrated and less inclined to see things in black-and-white terms.

He has less patience with alternatives. He once considered a myriad of choices before making any important decision; now he wants quick either/or resolutions. He can concentrate on only one thing at a time and acts more slowly than he once did. He gets upset quickly when, because of the partial paralysis of his vocal chords, he cannot make himself easily understood. After a while he learned to use this as an excuse whenever he lost his temper, even when it seemed to us that he was angry about something entirely different.

He occasionally accelerates his speech as if he were pressed for time. This is especially likely to occur when he recites something by heart, like the *Kiddush*, or when he reads a lecture before an audience. The speed sometimes causes him to drop some of his words or run them together, especially at the end of a sentence. Haste (festination) is also evident in Moshe's handwriting—he declares he cannot keep up with the speed of his thoughts. As a result, he frequently writes words incompletely, leaving out letters.

❖

Moshe's stubborn streak is more pronounced than it used to be. It can be well nigh impossible to divert him from an intention he has formed. My guess is that this stubbornness has been vital for his return to life. A less insistent man might have given up on many occasions when the difficulties seemed insurmountable.

## Follow-up

On the first anniversary of his coronary bypass surgery, a beautiful summer day, Moshe got up and laid the breakfast table for the two of us. He loves to eat breakfast with me. Now that he sleeps later, we do this regularly. In honor of the day, he asked me for an egg; he is proud that his dietary restrictions are less stringent than formerly. He has put on fifteen pounds since he awoke from his coma, and his hair is full and wavy. He not only looks well but is well.

Moshe had a busy day. He traveled to the Old City and negotiated the numerous steep steps to the office on his own, without difficulty. Only six months ago he believed he would never be able to use this office again. In the afternoon, accompanied by Rachel and Shraga, he spent an hour and a half at a book fair in the Liberty Garden, which is close to our house.

The evening was a time for celebration. I had invited the Bensons to dinner. This dinner fulfilled one of the fantasies I had conjured up to raise my hopes in those dismal early months when Moshe lay in a coma. Unfortunately Dr. Davies, the anesthesiologist, was abroad and so could not join the party. But David, the immunologist who was my constant medical adviser and kept vigil with us during Moshe's operation, joined us for dinner with his wife, Judy. Moshe opened a bottle of champagne and we all drank a toast to his health, to celebrate a happy ending to a horror story.

Gone is the warning Moshe repeated to me before his operation: "You won't have me around much longer." He no longer anticipates his imminent death, knowing that his physical condition—heart, blood pressure, blood sugar—are very good. Instead of constantly being concerned about dying, he wonders whether he can postpone his retirement a few years.

Gone are the long hours of listlessness and boredom which Moshe tried desperately to fill with people. Now his days are hardly long enough for him to work on all his scholarly projects and to write his books. He will even broadcast some lectures on the Bible in the coming weeks, as he used to do. In his leisure time he still enjoys having company and seeing films or plays. Above all, he loves to take little Elisha on his lap and play with him.

Gone are the tantrums and verbal abuse which used to appear with very little provocation. I no longer need to weep. Instead Moshe is making me laugh again. How wonderful to be able to laugh together as in former days! With his tenacity, will, and drive for independence, Moshe has succeeded in returning to a meaningful and creative life, after battling against incredible odds—against what seemed to be a hopeless state of neurological devastation.

Moshe no longer has the same flair for numbers he used to have, but his arithmetic skills are sufficient for his daily needs. He cannot remember even the approximate price of goods or services for which he paid, tends to misplace objects more often than in former days, and cries when excited. But he continues to improve. So seen from a long-term perspective, Moshe has not had to pay an excessively high price for the tremendous trauma to which he was subjected.

❖

People frequently ask Moshe, "What is your first memory from the time when you regained consciousness?" He is quite unable to answer that question. Probably he was so confused in those early weeks out of coma that he could not absorb any events well enough to remember them. But he gradually learned from our telling and retelling what did happen during that time. Nowadays, he cannot distinguish his own recollections from what he was told.

All of us have been changed by the experience of the past few years. None of us will ever be able to take Moshe for granted again. And none of us will ever again be able to shrug off a small risk factor. After all, Moshe fell into the small-percentage category twice: once when he entered a coma after his cardiac surgery (there are no statistics for such a likelihood, although at least 2 percent of U.S. patients over sixty years are known to suffer from circumvascular accidents such as strokes—which often involve one to two days of coma—after bypass surgery), and once when he awakened from his coma. No wonder Tamara was frightened when a public health nurse tried to reassure her that a certain innoculation carried less than a 1 percent risk of evoking encephalitis in her baby. Who in our family will ever shrug off such a small risk again?

The other day Moshe took the last chocolate out of a box of candy.

"I also want something good," I complained.

"You have me," he smiled back.

How right he is!

Fifteen months after surgery Moshe participated in two international congresses, presenting historical surveys of biblical studies at the International Old Testament Congress and of Hebrew lexicographical studies at the European Congress of Lexicography. The second of these meetings took place in Zurich, where we made excursions by boat, coach, and rail. At Lucerne, Moshe insisted on taking the cable car up to the Titlis, which at three thousand meters is the highest mountain in central Switzerland. He walked up and down hills for several hours, through towns and mountain villages, though this required considerable effort on his part. He had no difficulty orienting himself in the cities even when he used public transport. He visited museums and made sure that we saw several plays, both in London, where we stopped for a week, and in Zurich. In London he spent two mornings in the library of the British Museum, as had always been his custom.

This was not a restful vacation; the days simply did not have enough hours for everything Moshe wanted to accomplish. His appetite for "doing" things seemed insatiable. I was reminded of Strether's injunction to Little Bilham in Henry James's *The Ambassadors*: "Live, live all you can; it's a mistake not to." In fact, Moshe spoke of wanting to travel to South Africa, South America, and Australia, where he had not yet been. It was as if he had to see the whole world and do everything now that he had returned to life. He seemed to lack the tranquility for taking it easy, though he read a number of novels, including Thomas Mann's *Magic Mountain*, with pleasure.

I was in charge of budgeting Moshe's time, so I was the one who had to put the brakes on. In no way did I want to be a spoilsport, but I had to make him face reality. I tried to avoid head-on collisions and often found humor a great help.

Moshe's main trouble on this journey was his forgetting where he had put such important articles as the keys to our suitcases (we had to saw open the padlocks) and our credit cards (I found them in the wallet where they belonged). Finally I announced my refusal to engage in a daily lost-property hunt during my vacations and we took precautions to prevent these daily "losses."

We spent a week in Switzerland with Yona and Jonathan, who served as our drivers for excursions they were careful to plan with Moshe. Yet from time to time Moshe, who had always been the family driver, expressed his opposition to "the children's being in charge." At other times he went to the opposite extreme and became quite passive. It was clear that we had to involve Moshe in activities in whatever ways possible (an automatic transmission car had already been ordered for him back home).

Even during his vacations, Moshe's mind was often occupied with planning his future work. He was weighing whether to write a German–Hebrew dictionary, a theology of the Jewish prayer book, or a continuation into the eighteenth century of his history of Jewish studies. He was thinking of the lectures and seminars that he would give again at the Hebrew University and Bar Ilan University when the academic year began in November (two months hence). He had undertaken to resume his full teaching load, which would have daunted many less traumatized men. It was clear that he envisioned no respite for himself. I realized anew that Moshe's work is his life. Through work he expresses his real self and achieves meaning and self-respect no less than the respect of those around him.

Moshe's work and his environment, which includes a loving family and affectionate friends and colleagues, are vital for his well-being

—far more so than for someone who has not been subjected to his terrible traumas. They serve as an anchor. Feeling secure, Moshe can live at his highest potential, rather than having to prove himself again and again in a strange environment.

## Why Did Moshe Recover?

Why did Moshe recover? All his doctors were of the opinion that the odds were heavily stacked against this possibility. After all, he suffered from a deep coma that developed into the vegetative state only thirteen days after his second operation.

The physicians presumably based their opinions on cases comparable to Moshe's, which were reported in the medical literature:

S. A. Jacobson, in his article "Protracted unconsciousness due to a closed head injury" (*Neurology*, vol. 6, 1956), wrote about five patients who remained unconscious for a long time after head injury. Three were in a vegetative state after a month. The other two later recovered speech. One regained a vocabulary of only ten words. The other was able to verbalize requests but was wheelchair-bound, aggressive, and dependent on others.

A study by C. A. Carlsson and his colleagues called "Factors affecting the clinical course of patients with severe head injuries" (*Journal of Neurosurgery*, vol. 29, 1968), found that no one of Moshe's age who remained in a coma for more than six days recovered.

In the late 1960s Fred Plum and Jerome B. Posner published *The Diagnosis of Stupor and Coma* (F. A. Davis, 3d ed., 1981). They followed up five hundred comatose patients on both sides of the Atlantic and found that, of the twenty-four patients who remained in a vegetative state for more than two weeks, only five were alive at the end of the year. Three of these never recovered from the vegetative state. The other two had "overwhelming neurologic limitations as well as incapacitating mental impairments."

According to Plum and Posner, only one reasonably well-documented report of a dramatic recovery has appeared in medical sources, published by G. A. Rosenberg and colleagues: "Recovery of cognition after prolonged vegetative state" (*Annals of Neurology*, vol. 2, 1977). The patient remained in a vegetative state for a full year. For the first six months he neither opened his eyes nor reacted to noxious stimuli. Then he began to speak and follow commands. After two years he scored 100 on the verbal section of the Wechsler scale, indicating average intelligence. However, he was paralyzed in three extremities and totally dependent.

Plum and Posner reported a study of 110 chronically vegetative patients. Only 3 percent survived for three years, and none was able "to resume activity as a social human being" (p. 340).

Dobrokhotova (*Journal of Neuropathology and Psychiatry*, published in Russia and quoted in *Psychological Abstracts*, 1986) concluded, "At the current state of medical science the maximum duration of coma with the possibility of subsequent full recovery of mental activity in a patient under 30 years is 11 days."

On the basis of these reports and studies, Moshe had absolutely no chance of a recovery that would enable him to conduct a normal life. The literature suggested that if he remained alive, he would be left permanently in a vegetative state.

In line with this dismal prognosis went the story related to us by Mrs. Berndt, a well-wisher of Moshe's who lives in Berlin. She had visited him in the chronic geriatric ward after his awakening. To her question "How are you, professor?" he had answered, in German, "Beschissen" (Shitty). On her return to Berlin, she contacted a well-known professor emeritus of neurology, told him about Moshe's prolonged coma, and asked him to fly to Jerusalem at her expense to try to help Moshe recover. He replied that he did not want to waste her money: his long experience told him that no patient who had been comatose for so long had the slightest chance of regaining significant cognitive functioning or of achieving independence in daily living.

Mercifully, I was not entirely aware of how hopeless Moshe's situation was considered to be during his prolonged coma and vegetative state. By association, a scene in Chekhov's *Uncle Vanya* rises from the depths of my memory. Sonia, deeply in love with Astrov, has almost no hope that he returns her love. Yeliena, her young stepmother, offers to ask Astrov about it.

> *Yeliena:* All we want is to find out whether it's yes or no . . .
> *Sonia* (in great agitation): You will tell me the whole truth?
> *Yeliena:* Yes, of course. I think it's better to know the truth whatever it may be—it's not so dreadful as being kept in ignorance . . .
> *Sonia:* . . . no, ignorance is better. At least there is some hope.

I feel sure now that I retained hope because of my ignorance of Moshe's true prognosis.

But does anyone really know to what extent ischemic brain damage (damage due to insufficient blood supply to the brain) is reversible? Presumably some cases in which comatose patients have recovered are unreported in the medical literature. Are such cases indeed so rare, or are they overlooked because no one has bothered to write them up in the appropriate medical journals? They may be overlooked because scientists (including physicians) prefer to write about a large number of subjects or patients, so that they can apply statistical evaluations.

Single cases of recovery from coma are reported in the newspapers from time to time. During one six-week period in late 1986, four such stories came to my notice. Two, reported in local Israeli newspapers, were about patients who awakened from comas lasting seven weeks and eighteen months, respectively. The other two, reported in *Time* magazine and the Paris *Herald Tribune*, told of patients who regained consciousness after comas of five weeks and eleven years, respectively. Moreover, I was recently told about an eighty-year-old woman who, after three months in a deep coma (following surgery for removal of her gall bladder), slowly recovered when taken off the life-support system. A year later, she not only lived alone but also did her own shopping, cooking, and entertaining. She used a cane only when she was walking in the street. She even drove a car! Such stories indicate there may be more reason for hope than doctors ordinarily allow.

❖

Perhaps our constant stimulation of Moshe helped him return to us. We repeatedly told him how much we loved and missed him; we filled him in on daily events; we assured him that he was getting better all the time and that he would finally be well. Alon said these things out of a deep religious faith, whereas Jonathan and I wavered in our belief. Had Jonathan and I not been constantly reassured that comatose patients sometimes recover—several tales of dramatic recoveries were transmitted to us by Dr. Benson and others—we might not have been able to talk to Moshe with such conviction. One of the physicians later mentioned that he believed our "irrational belief " was responsible for Moshe's awakening. But we never thought we were being irrational in not giving up on Moshe.

We charted Moshe's progress. This helped indicate to us tangibly that improvement was likely to continue, even if not in a straight line. We knew this often meant two steps forward and one back, but at least we continued to see progress. We felt we had an advantage over the physicians who saw Moshe only occasionally, as if in stills—*we* saw his progress in motion. This was probably the reason the doctor in the acute geriatric ward, upon meeting Moshe for the first time, predicted that he would never leave the hospital.

A friend claimed that to understand why Moshe recovered one has to look for factors that are not really tangible. He referred to the human connection, "the network of support and the proximity of the family, people with whom Moshe was viscerally associated and where the sense of support and being with his own can be felt through the pores, when his brain was not working." If such factors are really crucial, perhaps they may be analyzed and quantified one day through research.

My mother's physician in London felt certain that the unconventional medication he had recommended, Nootropil, helped to stimulate Moshe's nerve cells and to increase the blood supply to his brain. The doctors at Hadassah did not think so. There have not yet been any controlled experiments on the efficacy of this drug.

Perhaps natural healing took place in a person of superior pretraumatic functioning who, with time, and (dare I say it?) luck, made a spontaneous recovery. This would then be similar to the case of "Donald" described by Oliver Sacks in *The Man Who Mistook His Wife for a Hat* (pp. 161–165).

Or perhaps intact parts of Moshe's brain were able to substitute for and accomplish the same functions as the damaged brain structures. Such intact parts of the brain had been less utilized or simply nonfunctional until then.

Believers in God found no difficulty in answering the question why Moshe recovered. Leaving aside the manner of God's intervention, they insisted that God had heard our prayers. Moshe's recovery was a miracle that had little or nothing to do with modern medicine and the application of heroic measures of care. Anyway, they claimed, the doctors did no more than maintain Moshe—they merely allowed him to make the recovery in his own time and way. Moshe's physicians spoke of a "medical miracle," by which they probably meant "a highly unusual event," although some of them added that Moshe appeared to be specially favored by God.

In a similar vein, one of Moshe's colleagues in Boston wrote: "Providence kept good watch over you, knowing full well that your job needs to be done."

The question why Moshe recovered remains open. It may have been, as his doctors maintained, a medical miracle. Alon is convinced that Moshe was spared by God. I do not know the answer. But I would like to find out whether our stimulation of Moshe helped in any way to propel him out of his vegetative state. Surely if the answer is yes, others could be advised to follow our example. Only research will be able to provide a more definitive answer.

## To Sue or Not To Sue

No sooner did the idea of bringing a malpractice suit occur to me than I dismissed it from my mind. Later, my American friends asked me whether I considered sueing for negligence. Rodney, with whom I discussed the operation, assured me that the complication of a leaking valve was totally unpredictable. And even if it could have been predicted, it could not have been prevented.

I was grateful that Moshe was alive and felt he needed all the good will of his doctors. They needed to do their utmost to help him get well. I did not wish to turn them into adversaries in a lawsuit. Nor could I afford to expend my energies on such an undertaking. I needed to devote every ounce of my energy and every moment of my time to Moshe's recovery and to retaining my own equilibrium. The possibility of winning money in a lawsuit was insignificant compared to these considerations.

After Moshe was back at home I was reassured to learn that negligence as defined by Israeli law did not apply in his case. In legal language, "negligence consists of failing to use such skill or to take such care in the exercise of a profession as a reasonable prudent person qualified to exercise such a profession would in the circumstances use." I had no reason to doubt that Moshe's doctors had used all their professional skills and had taken the utmost care to get him through his operation. In fact, I was convinced that without their skill and care Moshe would not have survived his surgery.

I learned only recently that in most American hospitals Moshe would not have been operated on to remove his hematoma in his comatose state. The doctors would have refused to intervene under such circumstances and Moshe would have died.

Moreover, according to The New York Times of October 17, 1987, the American Medical Association declared that it was ethical for doctors to withhold life-prolonging medical treatment, including food and water, from people in irreversible comas. Moshe's coma was regarded as irreversible. A court order in the United States might have required that life-prolonging medical treatment be withheld from him.

# Postscript

MOSHE GOSHEN-GOTTSTEIN

The weeks preceding and following my operation, as well as the resulting state of coma, were mercifully wiped out of my memory. I
cannot even say whether I heard or understood anything subliminally
or whether all my present knowledge of that time is the result of what
I found out later on.

One point, however, I can make: I never felt myself suspended
above my body or instructed by some supernatural power. Hence I
cannot tell any horticulturist what it feels like to be a "vegetable," as
I was termed.

I am happy that the doctors came to the conclusion that my brain
was not dead but only injured. Nobody could tell how much of my
brain had been affected and whether normal functioning would ever
be resumed. I am especially grateful that nobody decided that my life
support system should be turned off, or else this story would never
have been written.

I feel satisfied that my old joke stood the test: From a philologist
you can expect little good, but at least his mistakes are never life-
threatening. Whatever his mistakes, he cannot be proved wrong. A
physician, however, must be prepared to eat his own words, and even
his hat.

Though I am a practicing Jew, I look with incredulous eyes at the
idea that reciting psalms or changing my name was meaningful for
my recovery. Everything was tried to invoke a divine miracle, even
the last resort of one of our old friends, a former Jesuit priest, to have
a mass said on my behalf.

But I still am at a loss to comprehend the ways of God. Why did
this happen? I cannot see myself in the role of Abraham or Job, both
of whom underwent divine trials. Why this sudden blow and then
the miraculous return? I do not suffer from such hubris as to assume
that the Almighty himself devised this illness as a trial of our belief
or as his specific form of punishment for us.

Sometimes I wish I could afford the luxury of nonbelief. But is my belief merely a comforting delusion? Are my previous lifestyle and hereditary disposition reasons enough to explain what happened? Or should I rather become extrapunitive and blame the doctors and nurses for their possibly inadequate medical and nursing skills? Or should I end up in a dispute with God?

Many people refer to me today as a living miracle. And indeed, my recovery is a miracle unexplained by professionals. If there are any lingering aftereffects—apart from occasional congestion of the liver or lungs, because of a surplus of body fluids—these are psychological rather than physical.

For instance, my former tendency to extroversion has been lowered drastically. Nowadays, I find it hard to initiate a topic of conversation even with friends, and when I find myself the center of attention, as at last year's ceremony for the awarding of the Israel Prize, I am ill at ease.

My memory of the events leading up to the hospitalization remains rather fuzzy. I only remember feeling a heavy pressure in my chest as I tried to walk up the hill after the theater performance. Obviously something was very, very wrong, judging by the reactions of those around me. But my self-esteem did not allow me to become the object of self-pity.

I remember little of my state from the time I arrived back at home that fateful evening until I entered the operating room. I dimly recall sitting up in my hospital bed in the coronary ward and putting the final touches to my lecture for the forthcoming World Congress of Jewish Studies, as if that were the most important issue at that moment. Eventually I had to miss my lecture, and my son Alon read that paper in my stead. For some of the listeners, who by that time had heard of my state, it must have seemed as if a ghost were speaking out of his grave.

When I read that paper after it was printed in the proceedings of that congress, I could not even recall that I had written it in those painful days.

Whereas I cannot take responsibility for what I did while in the coma, I must acknowledge some responsibility for the demands I placed on my family after my return to life. Subconsciously I acted as if the world owed me a debt.

In the beginning I was interested only in myself. That attitude expressed itself, inter alia, in my refusal to wait in line. I would straightaway jump to the head of the line, waving my cane as justification of my behavior. It took me some time to realize what social behavior demands. I often put unreasonable demands on my assistants and secretaries when I felt that their work was not fast enough. I cannot understand today why they put up with me. After all, their remuneration is not excessive.

And now a few personal remarks as to how I see myself within my family circle. Pride of honor goes to Esther, on whom I depend today more than ever. Not only has she shared three and a half decades with me, with all their joys and troubles, but it was mainly she who looked after me while I was unconscious and bore the brunt of my aggression during my slow awakening. I have to plead innocence, because in the kind of injury I had sustained, aggression is apparently a common reaction, and Esther was the obvious target for it. This must have seemed the unkindest cut of all. Today I blush to think of what I did and said. But at least my aggression was a sign to those who loved me that I was regaining consciousness.

I am particularly ashamed to read of my cursing. The exclamation "Jesus, Maria, and Joseph" had no association or significance for me other than that I had heard it in Berlin when I was a child. (It was a typical expletive used by Berliners.) I did not realize that such exclamations would be regarded as blasphemous by Gudrun, the German nurse. Only when she asked me whether I had been a professor of New Testament studies did I realize that something was wrong. I learned never to use such swear words in her presence again.

Happily, no one understood my *Atta unsara*, Gothic or Old German for *Vater unser* ("Our father," which continues "which art in Heaven"). Had Gudrun heard this, she might have fainted.

I now know that Esther managed to keep a stiff upper lip, helped by our two sons. They neglected their own women and studies in order to stay by their father's side. They failed in nothing I might have wanted them to do. Their love cannot be repaid.

Fortunately both our sons had learned English and German and could therefore understand me when I used these languages. I now realize what happened to my erstwhile professor, N. H. Torczyner (Tur-Sinai), one of the pioneers of modern Hebrew, who had declared German a forbidden language in his household and never allowed his children to speak it even before their emigration to Palestine. In his old age he became senile and could speak only the Viennese German of his youth. His children had difficulty understanding him.

My languages returned in a gradual fashion—German first, Hebrew second, English third. Only much later could I quote from Latin or use Arabic and French. My Italian never reappeared, but then it was the weakest.

At the start of my coma Alon was already married to Tamara and Elisha was three months old. Alon had to deprive his own family to look after his father. Though a daughter-in-law cannot be expected to behave like a daughter, I can only say that when I came round I felt as if Tamara were my natural daughter. As for Jonathan, he was then in the process of courting Yona. One day he took her along to the hospital, and we have loved each other ever since. Yona acted all the time as if she were already part of our family. I cannot say to what extent I was a disturbing factor in the lives of the young couples.

Once I started thinking about my state I could understand what it must have meant to Job not to have had his children at his side to share his plight with him.

There was one positive aspect to my going through that hell: I became aware of the concern and warmth of my friends and colleagues. I was overwhelmed by the continuous flow of visitors. My bedside became a veritable Mecca. From whatever part of the world they came, they hugged and kissed me to express their happiness at seeing me. I had often evaluated people wrongly, but now gold proved to be gold.

The most golden of all were my assistants for the dictionary, Shraga and Rachel. I felt ashamed to accept so much help from them. They visited me daily and kept me company, taking turns sitting with me. Rachel did some intuitive occupational therapy with me, bringing a stack of slips with definitions of words for my dictionary, each of which I had to evaluate. Only much later did I find out how she reported back to Esther that my brain functioned as before, since accomplishing the dictionary work had been my major aim for decades. If one can respond to a rare word with a proper definition or a rare quote, it is a sign that the memory is functioning.

When I returned home my library was in disorder, my files had been mislaid, and my teaching schedule had to be put into order. Again I relied on Rachel and Shraga to put things right.

Rodney, our Bostonian doctor-friend, was a godsend who proved to be ever available to look after my health and to offer my family support. He even accompanied me on one of my first appearances at synagogue. He was the ideal doctor, behaving like a *Mensch,* a human being, first and only then as a doctor, without thereby losing his medical stature. It was extremely fortunate that he lived in our house precisely when I needed a private cardiologist.

In fact, he happened to be around at most of my subsequent health crises when his cardiological skills were needed. Coincidence or providence? Who can tell? He realized that once I left the hospital I was emotionally labile, tending to weep whenever the subject of my illness came up. He explained to me that I need not be ashamed of crying, since that kind of reaction is usual with people who have undergone an experience like mine.

I would be ungrateful if I did not say a few words about Dr. "Benson," my cardiac surgeon. Again, my memories of our first encounter disappeared in the extensive wipeout of those days. So I can write only from hearsay and from my later meetings with him. Dr. Benson was always ready with help and advice and never complained about Esther's early morning calls before he left home to operate on other patients. Bypass operations are nowadays routine procedures; my ending up in a comatose state was highly unusual and must have led to Dr. Benson's special relationship toward us. The explanation for the coma which we heard afterward was that, as sometimes happens, I had my first heart attack while on the operating table. Nobody can put the blame on the surgeon or the anesthetist. It would not be fair to ask in hindsight whether I would have been better off had my angina pectoris allowed me to be transported to the United States for the operation (although, once my brain functioned again, such ques-

tions arose naturally). All in all, the help my family and I received
from the surgeon was the best one could hope for. And I should stress
that we have meanwhile become good friends with Dr. Benson.

The very fact of being discharged from the geriatric ward, which
very few ever leave, was laden with emotion for me, my family, and
the staff. They had looked after me for many months, enabling me
in the end to make regular home visits. At long last my family could
take me home with them. Of course, it was understood that I was in
need of some professional help to learn to readjust to normal life. I
was already able to write at my desk and to continue to work on my
books, but my walking was still severely restricted.

A physiotherapist came to the house to help me move my legs until
a place was found for me at a day hospital three mornings a week.
By that time I was already reengaged in my work, and perhaps it was
my impatience that prevented more success there.

Most of the patients in that facility were in a far worse state than
I was. I had to do physiotherapy for my left foot as well as some
occupational therapy. I was fully aware of my need for physiotherapy,
since my "drop foot" caused great difficulties. On the other hand, I
did not understand why adult people should pass around a ball or
solve geometrical puzzles or practice multiplication tables. Perhaps I
was not ready to have the occupational therapist show me how badly
I functioned regarding space and numbers. Moreover, at that very
time the Israeli currency system had been changed and I had unusual
difficulties getting used to handling money.

All this taken together made me want to leave the day hospital as
soon as possible. Toward the end of my attendance there, I felt confident enough to try to drive a car again. Although I had driven a car
for decades, that skill also needed relearning. It was hard for me to
be told by the driving teacher to stay in the right lane, to drive more
slowly, and to follow the traffic signs exactly. I assume all that was
necessary in my state, but it did not help reinstill self-confidence.

The only positive aspect of all of this was that I had to get rid
of my old standard car and buy a new automatic-transmission, air-
conditioned car for the first time in my life. It is still unpleasant to
hear certain people wonder aloud whether I am able to drive all right,
in this country of notoriously bad drivers!

A few imperfections still bother me, and I react with abnormal vehemence if somebody treats me as handicapped. I have never regained the full use of my left foot (so that I have to use a cane outside), nor of some fingers on my left hand. This is rather bothersome whenever I want to run to catch a bus or when I try to type. But then I might have remained in a wheelchair for the rest of my life.

A much more embarrassing impediment still plagues me. Since I had a tube down my throat for a long time, my vocal cords apparently were damaged. When I had to deliver a lecture during my sabbatical year in 1987–88 before a large audience at New York University and could not manage to project adequately, Esther felt that remedial speech therapy was indicated. This meant that I had to relearn how to speak properly, without lowering my voice toward the end of sentences. For the rest of my sabbatical year in America, I went for speech therapy twice weekly. For someone who used to pride himself on his perfect articulation and who at the beginning of his academic career used to teach elocution, this impediment was most unpleasant. Therefore, I tried to deny its existence for a long time.

I realize that all these impediments could have been much worse and the damage more permanent. But recognizing something does not guarantee that one accepts it without feeling upset about it.

Among my friends and colleagues I have always had the reputation of putting more work on my plate than anybody could manage. Suggest to me a subject of research in my field or an entry in an encyclopedia and I jump to it regardless of other existing deadlines. Ask me for a contribution to a jubilee or memorial volume and I promise to write it. Bearing in mind my main projects, this attitude can lead to serious overwork.

There are even now more projects I still have to finish than ten healthy men can undertake. The major scholarly edition of the Hebrew Bible and the great dictionary of modern Hebrew could supply work for two academies, let alone side projects like the Arabic–Hebrew dictionary, the Jewish biblical theology, the grammar of modern Hebrew, and the history of Hebraic learning in humanist Europe. I fear that some of these plans will eventually come to a screeching halt.

Any hyperactivity can have pathological ingredients. The events since my illness have heightened my hyperactivity. I feel very much like someone granted a new lease of life, but certainly not immortality. How should I best husband my strength without wasting it on unimportant matters?

Four years after the operation, I feel embarrassed when people inquire about my state of health. I defend myself with a cynical "Terrible, thank God," which is intended to take the kind inquirer aback. As far as I am concerned, my state of health is as good as that of the next fellow and I feel I can undertake anything, even though from time to time I get a small reminder of my previous illness.

My walking difficulty might have restrained my inveterate appetite for travel abroad. Passing through airports can be difficult even for normal travelers. Yet last year (in the summer of 1988) I insisted on traveling back from my sabbatical in the United States via New Zealand, Australia, and the Far East, a plan which seemed exciting even if somewhat adventurous. Some well-meaning friends raised their eyebrows and wondered why Esther allowed such a crazy venture. Of course without her I could not have embarked on it. But ultimately I did everything possible from flying in a one-engine plane over the fjords of New Zealand to exploring the caves in Australia, to climbing up the steps of temples in Bali. Perhaps I had to prove to myself that in spite of my handicap I would not forgo the activities in which others engage. I would have been very upset had I listened to the prophecies of doom and given up my travel plans. Only recently (July 1989) I have returned from inaugurating a chair for Jewish theology and philosophy at Frankfurt University. I cannot say whether I mention all this in order to boast or to describe my feeling that if I do not manage to accomplish what I want now I will never be able to do so.

Of course before I decide to go abroad, I always consult my cardiologist. If he warns me that a certain type of trip might prove dangerous for me, I very reluctantly give it up—as happened this summer when I wanted to go to Turkey and was strongly advised against it.

I should like to mention at least a few events that were of special significance to me. Long before the operation, I had planned to convene an international group of scholars in one of my fields of interest to join me in Jerusalem at our Institute for Advanced Studies. When the time came, I was still a patient in the chronic geriatric ward. Once the group had assembled in Jerusalem, I sent them my regrets for not being able personally to extend my welcome as a host to them—whereupon the entire group came to my hospital ward. The thoughtful administrator put the entire dining area at our disposal. Subsequently, she admitted how touched she felt that the group had made a "pilgrimage" to her "star" patient and had discussed serious issues with him.

That hospital ward was arranged for the care of old people whose behavior is often unusual and unfit for company. Thus, when I awoke from the coma, I found myself surrounded by elderly, decrepit people, often strapped to their wheelchairs, babbling and rocking, sometimes even shouting and cursing—a picture that seemed lifted right out of Dante's *Inferno*. Was I condemned to spend the rest of my days in such company? Moreover, the bars attached to my bed to prevent me from falling out made me think I was in prison.

But I prefer to continue with the bright side of those days. Once I was out of the hospital, Yona and Jonathan decided to make their engagement public. They had waited to do so until I had fully come round. It was a match of which any parent would have been happy to approve. Thus I gained another daughter-in-law who meanwhile has become a mother and a full-fledged lawyer.

So I feel that with all its joys and pains, life goes on normally as if nothing had happened.

The most unexpected special event during the past year occurred halfway through my sabbatical in the United States. I received a phone call from Mr. Itzchak Navon, the Israeli minister of culture, who informed me that he had just confirmed the choice of the academic nominating committee to award me the Israel Prize for Jewish Studies on the occasion of the fortieth anniversary of the state. He wanted me to come home on Independence Day to collect the prize. The annual Israel Prize, when given to someone in my field, is the nearest to the Nobel Prize, as one Nobel laureate pointed out to me when he met me later. No wonder that after the hell I had been through this felt like heaven.

At this point, I should like to recount a few dreams which may perhaps disclose the state of my mind after I recovered consciousness and was still in the hospital. Even now they appear vividly before me. Unfortunately, I cannot recollect the order in which I dreamed them.

I try to cross a stretch of water in order to get home but no ship is in sight. I cry for someone to have pity on me and get me across the water.

I have money but cannot get to it. My annoyance grows because I put it into some account which I cannot get at. An acquaintance of mine, the bank director who visited me in the hospital, arranges for me to overdraft my account since I have money to defray the overdraft.

I am in a home where a Friday evening meal is being served. Some woman hands out the dinner to her children. One child does not get all the different kinds of food. Is it me?

I go to synagogue on the Sabbath. We are invited for a meal. First Kiddush is made by one of the participants. Why not me?

We, the patients, are being cleaned by a male nurse. This is very unpleasant because it means being taken into the bathroom in a wheelchair and then splashed all over. I decide to ask a female nurse whether she could wash me in a more pleasant way.

While female nurses uncover me in the morning—which I find most unpleasant—to see if I am clean and dry from the night, I am studying a catalogue of Ethiopian manuscripts intensely. (I had not pursued the study of such manuscripts for decades.)

One element common to all these dreams is a state of discomfort and forlornness.

❖

Who am I today? The same Moshe I was before, the same husband and family man, the same scholar and teacher? After an event such as I have experienced, these questions are very pertinent. Is the urge to travel and meet different people part of that picture? Altogether, is the picture I draw of myself too harsh or too lenient? Will my story interest anybody?

I realize today how close I was to remaining a vegetable for the rest of my life. Looking back at the events since my operation, I feel that I pulled through in spite of the prognosis of the doctors. Yet I cannot complain about the medical experts—they did what they could for me. In the final instance, I believe that my recovery was due not only to the mercy of God but also to my family and friends, who refused to surrender hope. That was the real miracle.

# Appendix A
*Child Development and Recovery from Coma*

The reader will probably be surprised by my juxtaposition of two such seemingly disparate topics as child development and recovery from coma. Could there possibly be any similarity between these two? I would like to give an account of how I came to see the similarity.

Since I had a young grandchild when Moshe was coming out of the coma, it was almost inevitable that I should compare their development. Moreover, once Moshe was on his way to recovery, I often found myself speaking to him as if he were a young child. I used the first person plural—"Now we are going to have lunch," rather than "You are going to have lunch"—and I used diminutive terms like *Stühlchen* (little chair) instead of *Stuhl* (chair) when I spoke to him in German. Only his clear resentment at being addressed in this way made me aware of what I was doing.

Why did I behave like this? In Moshe's prolonged state of unconsciousness, he was totally dependent on others for his most basic needs. Babies are also totally dependent creatures. So an association began to form in my mind and, once formed, was not easily relinquished. Indeed, I noticed many similarities between an infant's development and Moshe's behavior upon coming out of coma.

- Moshe was very labile. His emotions changed rapidly, as do an infant's. He cried easily, and when he laughed it seemed out of proportion to what the situation warranted. He changed his mind from moment to moment: Once he reacted violently to my suggestion that I open a can of tuna for him, but a minute later he asked me to go ahead and open the can.
- His needs were very insistent and had to be satisfied immediately. He would not take no for an answer. He could not wait for the elevator to arrive or to get a word in at the table. Babies want their food at once partly because they have no sense of time. Did Moshe lack a sense of time? I cannot tell. However, Moshe's needs were

more often social than physiological (except one Sabbath at home, when he insisted that he must have ice cream).

During those early weeks Moshe was highly narcissistic, interested only in himself. It appeared that he had to invest all his energies in himself in order to recover. Other people and their needs did not really concern him. When he wanted Jonathan or me by his side, it did not matter to him that Jonathan had exams or that I was seeing patients.

• Moshe's impulse control was poor at first. He became upset when his wishes were not granted or when he felt misunderstood, and he threw tantrums very like a young child. But whereas a young child often needs to be physically held and controlled in order to simmer down, Moshe's tantrums tended to blow over if we ignored them and did not react.

• Soon after he awakened from his coma, Moshe, like an infant in the first six months of life, seemed unable to differentiate himself from other people. When the patient in the bed next to his died, he was convinced that he himself had died. Of course, his helplessness led him to draw this conclusion more easily.

• Moshe's mood was dependent on sufficient sleep. Without it he tended to become easily upset, querulous, even tearful. Often a nap had a restorative function as it does for an infant or toddler.

• Soon after Moshe emerged from coma his food intake was connected to my person: he refused to eat because he wanted to annoy me. In this respect he was like a young child who is locked in conflict with the mother. By refusing to eat, the child seems to say, "I don't want you or anything from you."

• After the first few weeks out of coma, Moshe did not want the boys or me to leave him. He did not consider Alon a worthy substitute for me. I asked myself whether Moshe, like a baby at the end of the first year of life and the beginning of the second, lacked "object permanence." Was he able to appreciate that other people and things have an existence of their own, independent of whether he saw them or not? However, Moshe did not appear to be anxious when we were absent, as an infant would be. He merely felt better in our presence and therefore demanded it. "You are not supposed to leave, you don't go," he often said, like a child who makes his or her parents feel guilty when they go out. But in this case it was the children and I who were made to feel guilty.

• Moshe could not occupy himself when we were away from him—neither at the hospital, where he demanded constant visitors, nor at home, where a professional caretaker could not substitute for me. Young children may also be unable to play when their mothers or mother substitutes are absent.

• Like a young child who holds the mother responsible for pains and unpleasant feelings because she is present when the child suffers from them, Moshe blamed me for his predicament.

• In a young child, aggression alternates with positive feelings; the child is frequently playful. But when Moshe came out of his coma, the serious intent behind his aggression and the lack of humor accompanying it made it seem frightening. Whereas a child frequently uses curses to test parents' reaction, Moshe used expletives in deadly earnest for a long time. Only later did he use blasphemous language and "naughty" behavior to test his environment.

• Moshe's negativism, similar to that of a two-year-old, established his individuality and separateness from me, proving that he had a will of his own.

• Moshe desperately needed to regain his independence, but he also wanted to remain dependent. For example, he did not want me to interest myself in "his domain" but, on the other hand, demanded that I cut his meat. Gradually I had to let him resume his former responsibilities like dressing himself, writing checks, and preparing his own breakfast. In fact, I had to struggle not to become overprotective toward him.

I learned from experience that praise for achievement is not always desirable with adults, though it is usually necessary with children. My praising Moshe for using the toilet was humiliating to him. He must have thought I was making fun of him.

• Moshe's speech development started not with babbling but with nonsense words, followed by meaningful words and sentences. However, while a young child voices meaningful words within a particular context (for instance, saying "cat" when he or she sees one), usually none of us could fathom *why* Moshe said *what* he said *when* he said it. It did not seem to be in reaction to any external event.

• A young child takes many weeks or months to move through each stage of development. Moshe's development was much more rapid. He used the toilet regularly less than a week after emerging from coma, except for occasional accidents; he walked upstairs with alternate feet as soon as he started climbing stairs. Small children start negotiating stairs by climbing onto each step with both feet. And of course he did not go through a period of crawling prior to standing up and walking.

Stimulation is the main issue here, and I have left it to the end in order to try to do it justice. Did stimulation help to get Moshe out of his coma? The analogy with child-rearing was obvious: as Dr. Daniel Stern points out in *The First Relationship: Infant and Mother* (1977), the infant needs stimulation to provide the brain with the raw materials required for maturation of the perceptual, cognitive, and sensorimotor processes, just as the body needs food to grow. It seemed to make sense that similar "brain food" would be necessary in order to extricate a comatose patient from coma.

Stern, however, stresses the fact that stimulation must be adapted to the child's state. Imposing stimulation arbitrarily (without considering, for instance, whether the child is fully awake) leads to no improvement in developmental test scores because a given infant may not be able to assimilate such stimulation. The amount, kind, and timing of stimulation must be closely related to the infant's own psychological organization. The parents must allow themselves to be paced by the baby. A mutual feedback system is established whereby parents and child adjust their behavior to one another. But the parents usually adapt their behavior to the child's needs. Stimulation has to occur when the child is most alert, and it has to be appropriate for his or her age.

Unfortunately, there can be no mutual feedback system where a comatose patient is concerned. When I spoke to Moshe or smiled at him, I had no alert partner. I therefore could not adjust my behavior to him, nor was he capable of signaling to me that he was being inundated by excessive stimulation—he could neither turn away nor cry. I did not know when to intervene, since Moshe was incapable of spontaneous behavior. Owing to Moshe's comatose state, change could not come from within a relationship between us. However, once Moshe regained consciousness, all stimulation had to be closely related to his state. He became able to avoid excessive stimulation either by turning away or by protesting. In turn, we could provide stimulation or protect him from excessive doses of it.

# Appendix B
## Advice to Those in a Similar Situation

Time and again I have been asked to give a prescription for getting a loved one out of his or her coma. My first response has always been that if I had such knowledge I would deserve a Nobel Prize. Yet there are a few directions I would like to suggest. They can do no harm and may do much good. Without them the story I have told would remain merely a unique one, without application for those in a similar situation.

Don't give up on a loved one who is in a coma unless the patient is brain-dead or modern techniques of looking at brain structure (such as the CAT scan or magnetic resonance imaging) establish that serious destruction in the brain stem prevents such vital bodily functions as breathing. Neurologists cannot predict with complete certainty whether a coma is irreversible.

Your presence at the bedside makes the nursing staff try a little harder. And what do *you* have to lose by trying a little longer? You may antagonize doctors who want the bed for the next patient, but that is not *your* problem. Your concern is to do everything you can so that your loved one may regain consciousness.

Provide stimulation for the patient. In a letter to the *Lancet* dated July 15, 1978, E. B. LeWinn and M. D. Dimancescu speak of "a state of environmental deprivation in the comatose patient though his problem is primarily cerebral." In a pilot study of sixteen patients in severe coma (3 to 5 on the Glasgow coma scale), they provided intensely enriched environmental input. All sixteen patients recovered fully from their coma. Of a comparable group of fourteen patients who were not given programs of environmental enrichment, eleven died. These striking though unconfirmed preliminary results suggest that talking to comatose patients may actually save their lives.

John La Puma and colleagues (*Archives of Neurology*, vol. 45, 1988) point out that many comatose patients have physiological responses to auditory stimuli and may be able to hear. Their vital signs, such as heart and respiratory rates and intracranial pressure, change with auditory stimulation. The authors suggest that if doctors and family members do not talk to comatose patients, because they are unresponsive, those patients who can hear may come to believe that they are dead or nearly dead. Thus, not talking to them may become a self-fulfilling prophecy.

In view of these findings, I suggest that you proceed under the assumption that the patient can hear you and that your stimulation will help him or her to recover from the coma. Talk, read, and sing to him or her, play music, touch and stroke him or her, and, if you wish, pray at his or her bedside.

The very fact that you support your loved one may be of crucial importance. We know that in the presence of another person, one's cardiovascular signs improve, the immune system is stimulated to fight infectious disease, and the endorphins are activated. These beneficial results are achieved even if you only sit with someone who cannot interact. So your support may have a beneficial effect even on a comatose patient.

Believe in what you are doing. Seek out others who know or have heard of comatose patients awakening. Once you are able to detect even small signs of improvement, take note of them, follow them up, rejoice in them, and hope for more. But remember, progress often consists of two steps forward and one backward. Don't allow the inevitable regressions to depress you.

I have met two women whose husbands awakened from deep coma against their doctors' expectations. Each was at her husband's bedside every day, holding his hands, stroking him, speaking encouragingly to him, conveying her love in whatever way possible. My guess is that there are many more such cases and that the number could be greatly augmented.

Let me add two warnings, however:

I would be doing a disservice if I held out hope that everyone in a coma can recover consciousness if treated in this way. Unfortunately, many comatose patients never wake up, however much their families invest in them. But even in the event of the worst scenario, the family will at least be able to feel that they have tried to do everything humanly possible.

Recovery, if and when it does occur, will probably never be complete; residual problems and deficits will very likely remain, some of them quite serious. But when the patient emerges from coma, those who have persevered will feel privileged to witness—perhaps even to have facilitated—a return to life, a veritable rebirth.

❖

Parents may become so absorbed in their own pain that they cannot take adequate care of their children, who then effectively lose two parents. Even if you have no young dependent children, you need to be strong and competent. Try to serve as a model for your family on how to live in such circumstances. Don't let them worry about you, which would only add to their stress. But do not hesitate to share your suffering with them, thereby enabling them to express their own feelings.

Each family member must re-establish his or her own priorities and fulfill his or her own needs in addition to caring for the comatose patient. Do not risk burnout—physical and mental exhaustion due to long-term involvement in an emotionally draining situation. Therefore balance your personal needs and the patient's requirements for care. Encourage every family member to return to his or her personal and professional life as soon as the patient's state has stabilized.

It would be wrong to allow yourself to be overwhelmed by the situation or to become a martyr—wrong for your own mental well-being and for that of the rest of the family, since it would make them feel unnecessarily guilty. Therefore I suggest you augment your own emotional supplies by drawing on the support of your family and friends, by working part-time if possible, so as to feel efficacious in at least one area; by indulging in activities that give you pleasure in your spare time; and by expressing your doubts and anguish to people you can trust. After all, what you undertake will be far from easy. It may involve a long and arduous struggle that frequently appears to be hopeless, especially if the doctors continue to be discouraging. If you are a religious person, you may find prayer a great solace and comfort.

There are many ways in which you can try to keep misery from overwhelming you: Refuse to "catastrophize," to let anything upset you too deeply, to attach negative labels to any situation, to regard any event as a "bad omen," to compare your patient with those in a better state of health, to indulge in self-pity, and to think about memorable dates. Try to use humor as an antidote.

Stop yourself from dwelling on the worst possible prognosis. For me this was that Moshe would remain in a vegetative state permanently. I also dismissed other terrible possibilities from my mind—for instance, that I might become a kind of *agunah,* a deserted wife, who according to Jewish law can never marry again since she has not been divorced by her husband. After all, an unconscious husband cannot divorce his wife. Was I to be irrevocably anchored to this nonresponsive object? I dispelled such thoughts as soon as they welled up within me. Try not to let anything upset you deeply or for a long time, but do allow yourself to cry whenever the need arises. Teach yourself to ignore any incident that might annoy you under more normal circumstances, since you will not have the energy to become emotionally involved in minor matters. It is so easy to blow trivial issues out of proportion when everyone's nerves are on edge, so it requires a conscious effort to foster a good atmosphere, especially with the children.

My advice to avoid negative emotions in this situation is quite contrary to the attitude encouraged in psychotherapy. As a therapist, I encourage my patients to explore their feelings in depth and enable them to face their hostile emotions. This is often very hard for them and may lead to temporary regression. But in the circumstance of a family member's coma, the aim is not self-exploration. You must remain healthy in body and mind to cope with an objectively difficult situation day after day, without knowing when it will end. You have to conserve your energies for what is really necessary. If you allow yourself to become deeply upset, you will not be able to function adequately. For this reason you cannot afford to regress.

Try to stop yourself from attaching negative labels to situations. For example, during the second week after Moshe's operation, the thought crossed my mind as I walked to the hospital, "This is my Via Dolorosa, my path of suffering." As soon as I recognized what I was doing, I stopped it.

Returning home one evening after dinner with friends, I found the contents of all our closets emptied onto the beds. Burglars had entered through the garden, searched systematically for cash and gold, and disappeared with their loot. My first reaction was to panic, but Alon reassured me when I called him: "Compared with Dad's condition this is not so bad." He was right: nothing was shocking when viewed in that light. For a moment, I compared myself to Job. What else was in store for me? As soon as I realized that I had attached a negative label to the situation, I stopped it. In this way I was able to go on with daily living, unimpeded by the implications of identifying myself with Job.

Do not allow yourself to regard any incident as a bad omen. When you break or lose an object, particularly a significant one, at a time of great stress and uncertainty, it is difficult not to view it as a prophetic sign. When my watch stopped, I had to make a conscious effort not to associate this with Moshe's future. And when my household helper reported to me that she had lit a candle on behalf of Moshe at the Western Wall, but that the candle had quickly been extinguished, I told myself that this did not portend a misfortune.

A well-known example of an event construed as a bad omen is incorporated in a romantic legend about Mozart. A messenger is reported to have delivered an unsigned letter asking the composer to accept a commission for a requiem mass. The letter arrived at a time when Mozart's health and finances were failing. It is easy to understand why the notion arose that Mozart conceived his Requiem as a funeral mass for himself.

Do not compare your patient with healthier patients. It is easy to envy them and their families—or indeed to envy anyone who is leading a normal life. It is equally easy to indulge in self-pity, but that will do nothing but paralyze you.

You should purposely ignore special dates associated with the patient, such as wedding anniversaries and birthdays. I tried not to think about Moshe's sixtieth birthday, which occurred during his third month in the hospital. The family had planned a big celebration at which Moshe would be presented with a Festschrift to which his students had contributed. As it turned out, we all said "Happy Birthday" to him, but he seemed unaware of the significance of that day or indeed of any other day.

Humor is a wonderful antidote to misery. Keep your eyes open for the absurd and comical. I allowed myself an internal laugh when one of my patients asked if I knew what a coronary bypass operation was. I smiled at the absurdity of a friend who considered it inappropriate to visit me at home because she was dressed up to go to a wedding. When I invited friends at the time of the congress Moshe had helped to plan, I was glad to be able to laugh at the stories with which they regaled me, mainly, I am sure, to divert me at least during that one evening.

The above thoughts and techniques are intended to prevent you from drowning in a sea of misery. You will need all the strength and courage you can muster. My heart goes out to you.

## SELECTED READINGS

Calabrese, Joseph R., et al. Alterations in immuno-competence during stress, bereavement, and depression. *American Journal of Psychiatry* 144:9 (1987): 1123–1130.

Kiecolt-Glaser, Janice K., and Ronald Glaser. Psychological influences on immunity. *Psychosomatics* 27:9 (1986): 621–624.

La Puma, J., D. L. Schiedermeyer, A. E. Gulyas, and M. Siegler. Talking to comatose patients. *Archives of Neurology* 45(1988): 20–22.

LeWinn, E. B. The coma arousal. *Journal of the Royal Society of Health* 100 (1980): 19–21.

LeWinn, E. B., and M. D. Dimancescu. Letter to *Lancet.* 15 July 1978: 2, 156–157.

Lynch, James J. *The Broken Heart.* New York: Basic Books, 1977.

Schleifer, Steven J., et al. Behavioral and developmental aspects of immunity. *Journal of the American Academy of Child Psychiatry* 25:6 (1986): 751–763.

# Appendix C

*Unexplained Recovery from a Persistent*
*Vegetative State: A Physician's Viewpoint*

Rodney H. Falk, M.D., FACC

It is always difficult for a physician to treat a comatose patient whose prognosis is apparently hopeless. After a period of deep unresponsiveness, during which the patient appears to be in a deep, immobile sleep, eyelid opening and closing and eye movements often return, yet there is no evidence of any level of communication between the patient and his family or attendants. This level of coma, known as a persistent vegetative state, often gives the family a sense of false hope, since they may misinterpret random eye movements as purposeful attempts to communicate. When this occurs, repeated attempts by the (usually) dispassionate nursing or medical staff fail to reproduce the communication.

In my position as a cardiologist in an inner-city hospital with a busy emergency room I have all too often experienced the agonizing plight of families whose loved ones have been resuscitated from an out-of-hospital cardiac arrest in time to allow their hearts to function again but too late to allow their oxygen-starved brains to recover consciousness. The decisions faced by the family in such a situation are very difficult. Decisions about the aggressiveness of care or even about the termination of artificial ventilation ("life support") may have to be made, and family involvement is most important in these decisions. In my opinion it is the responsibility of the doctor to become involved with the family in these difficult times. This means making them aware of the reality of the situation while being sensitive to their needs and beliefs. All too often the physician has been in this situation many times before and fails to understand the agony and confusion of a family thrown into a high-technology medical world whose center is their close relative, so recently walking and talking. There are those physicians who put the burden of final decision-making on the family —whether to treat a pneumonia, when to perform cardiopulmonary resuscitation, and when to terminate life support. I firmly believe that it is the duty of every physician to make those decisions but to be heavily guided by the family's wishes so that they feel able to participate in the care. The doctor should listen carefully to the family and never attempt to terminate care prematurely against their wishes, even when the prognosis appears hopeless. Yet he or she should explain the medical facts in order to aid the family in their understanding. If a family member feels involved in patient care decisions, it lessens the frightening feeling of total loss of control and greatly improves doctor-family communication. But the reins should remain gently in the physician's hands so that when (as so often happens) a *mutual* decision to forgo further therapy is made, the family is not thereafter constantly tortured by the thought that they themselves had directly terminated the life of their relative.

My involvement with Moshe's case put me in an unusual position. He was a neighbor and had become, in the few months that my wife, infant daughter, and I had lived in the same apartment building, a good friend. He and his family had treated us with their warm hospitality and I, as a physician, had treated him when he was first hospitalized with angina. Although I was no longer directly involved with his care after surgery, I was intensely involved with his family and felt myself "in both camps." As a doctor I knew the grim outlook in such cases. As a family friend and confidant I felt the burning desire to clutch at every straw and to try every avenue to bring about a recovery.

The events of those months are movingly documented in this book. My contribution here is to put into perspective the medical facts which led me to believe at the time that the chances of meaningful recovery were hopeless and have led me subsequently to publish this case in the medical literature. The following is a summary of the case report which appears in the *Postgraduate Medical Journal*, which also briefly reviews relevant medical literature on this topic. The details of the case given in the medical report are omitted, as they are described fully in this book.

The prognosis of patients with coma has been a subject of detailed study in recent years. The persistent vegetative state—a condition with sleep-wake cycles and spontaneous eye opening but no consistent behavioral evidence of psychological interaction with the environment (Jennet and Plum 1972)—is a common condition following brain injury resulting from either oxygen deprivation or trauma. Not including the present case, only three cases of unexpected recovery from a persistent vegetative state have been published (Rosenberg et al. 1977; Shuttleworth 1983; Arts et al. 1985). In two of these cases severe residual defects remained, and the patients were unable to function independently. The third patient, a twenty-three-year-old graduate student, was in a vegetative state for seven weeks after carbon monoxide poisoning and then recovered sufficiently to lead a normal existence. She was unable to resume her studies, however, and remained mildly physically and intellectually impaired (Shuttleworth 1983).

In order to determine whether certain features of coma could predict subsequent recovery, an international study of over five hundred comatose patients in three major hospitals was undertaken (Levy et al. 1981). Two hundred and ten of these patients became comatose due to cerebral hypoxia or ischemia (lack of oxygen or blood flow to the brain) and many of these died within seven days (Levy et al. 1985). Of the thirty-three who were in a vegetative state at one week three regained independence. In contrast, of the fifteen patients vegetative at one month none ever became independent. All patients had standard clinical neurological tests performed early in their hospital course in an attempt to predict outcome. If after twenty-four hours of coma the pupils did not respond to light and the eyes did not blink when touched with a piece of cotton, independent recovery never occurred. Similarly, in the absence of purposive limb movements by seventy-two hours no patient ever recovered. Moshe's pupillary response returned only on day six and purposeful limb movements only in the fifth week of his coma. Thus, based on the data described by Levy and associates, his prognosis would have been judged hopeless at seventy-two hours. In many hospitals this would have been the decisive factor either in considering whether to discontinue ventilator support or to withhold antibiotic therapy if a pneumonia or other infection supervened.

Although Moshe's case is certainly out of the ordinary and inexpli-

cable, it raises certain important issues. Application of clinical algo-
rithms to predict coma outcome has been criticized on ethical
grounds and the applicability to individual patients of data derived
from large groups has been questioned (Black 1985). During the
course of Moshe's illness his family was extremely involved and insisted that all supportive measures be applied. Without this involvement it is unlikely that he would have survived several serious in-
fective episodes. Information on recovery from prolonged coma was
sought by the family and several such anecdotal cases were described
to them, but none had been documented in the medical literature.
These cases may not have been published because the details presented to the family were distorted or exaggerated, but it is possible
that some were indeed true recoveries from non-traumatic major cerebral insults. Clearly the publication of details of any such cases in
refereed medical journals is crucial to determine the frequency with
which recovery occurs and to examine any common factors in these
rare events. Perhaps an international registry of unexpected coma recoveries should be developed, which may give further insight into
hitherto poorly recognized physiological, pathological, and external
factors responsible for improvement in patients with coma (La Puma
et al. 1988).

Whatever the reasons for Moshe's miraculous recovery, his story
is a lesson in hope and in the marvelous devotion of a remarkable
family. It is also a lesson in humility to me as a physician. Although
I have never seen anything similar before or since (and I have experience of many such cases), it has altered my view of the word
"hopeless." In cases such as these, particularly early in the hospital
stay, many a family longs to be given a word of hope among the many
disheartening things they hear. While I always explain the most likely
outcome, mention of Moshe's recovery in an appropriate context can
soften the dreadful news until the family has had time to adjust to
the grim outlook that, almost inevitably, awaits their relative who has
remained deeply comatose for several days.

## REFERENCES

Arts, W. F. M., H. R. Van Dogen, J. Van Hof-Van Duin, and E. Lammens. Unexpected improvement after prolonged post-traumatic vegetative state. *Journal of Neurology, Neurosurgery and Psychiatry* 48(1985): 1300–1303.

Black, P. M. Predicting the outcome from hypoxic-ischemic coma: Medical and ethical implications. *JAMA* 254(1985): 1215–1216.

Jennet, B., and F. Plum. Persistent vegetative state after brain damage: A syndrome in search of a name. *Lancet* 1(1972): 734–737.

La Puma, J., D. L. Schiedermeyer, A. E. Gulyas, and M. Siegler. Talking to comatose patients. *Archives of Neurology* 45(1988): 20–22.

Levy, D. E., D. Bates, J. J. Caronna, et al. Prognosis of nontraumatic coma. *Annals of Internal Medicine* 94(1981): 293–301.

Levy, D. E., J. J. Caronna, D. H. Singer, R. H. Lapinski, H. Frydamn, and F. Plum. Predicting outcome from hypoxic-ischemia coma. *JAMA* 253 (1985): 1420–1426.

Rosenberg, G. A., S. F. Johnson, and R. P. Brenner. Recovery of cognition after prolonged vegetative state. *Annals of Neurology* 2(1977): 167–168.

Shuttleworth, E. Recovery to social and economic independence from prolonged postanoxic vegetative state. *Neurology* 33(1983): 372–374.

---

This contribution is based on my article "Physical and intellectual recovery following prolonged hypoxic coma," to appear in *Postgraduate Medical Journal*. Permission to use this material is gratefully acknowledged.

# Appendix D

## *Timeline*

| | |
|---|---|
| Moshe is hospitalized in Intensive Coronary Care Unit | June 4, 1985 |
| Bypass operation | June 24, 1985 |
| Second operation | June 27, 1985 |
| | |
| Opens right eye | 13 days after first operation |
| Opens left eye | 16 days after first operation |
| Moshe is now in vegetative state with wake–sleep cycles | |
| | |
| Moshe is moved to cardiac surgery ward | 4 weeks after operation |
| Moves right arm | |
| Moves right leg | 4½ weeks after operation |
| | |
| Moves left arm | 6 weeks after operation |
| Turns head to the side | |
| Holds head upright | |
| Follows moving objects with his eyes | |
| Moshe is now in coma vigil | |
| | |
| Moves left leg | 7 weeks after operation |
| Responds to handshake | |
| Shoos fly away from his chin | |
| | |
| Occasionally focuses on person who looks at him | 8 weeks after operation |
| | |
| Emits high vocal sound | 6 weeks after operation |
| | |
| Emits low vocal sound (groan) | 7 weeks after operation |
| Moves lips | |
| Whispers nonsense words | |
| Whispers "hand," "good," "ima" (mother) | |
| | |
| Repeats name of friend | 8 weeks after operation |
| | |
| "Water" and "Mayim" (Hebrew for *it*) | 9 weeks after operation |
| "I want to eat" | |

| | |
|---|---|
| Whispers 3–4-word sentences in German and Hebrew sentences from prayer | 10 weeks after operation |
| Shouts back words after we voice what he whispers | |

| | |
|---|---|
| Recites series of numbers in German | 11 weeks after operation |
| Responds "she is going" to my "I am going" | |

| | |
|---|---|
| Neighbor introduces himself by first name; Moshe adds his surname | 12 weeks after operation |
| Long German sentences | |
| Calls me by name | |
| Drinks tea by mouth | |
| Thanks someone for regards | |
| Gives his name correctly when asked | |
| Completes Hebrew prayers I intone on Rosh Hashanah | |
| Remembers first two verses of *She'ma* by heart | |
| Nods and shakes head as nonverbal communication | |
| Translates words from German into English and from Hebrew into German | |
| Turns himself in bed; arranges pillow under his head | |
| Swears vociferously, mainly in German | |
| Physically violent | |
| Plays ball glove game with Alon | |
| Tells Jonathan, "you are my son" | |
| Gives his age correctly | |
| "Ich will lesen" (I want to read) | |
| Reads short sentence in German | |
| "She wants to murder me"; "I'll murder you" | |

| | |
|---|---|
| Physical and verbal aggression increase | 14 weeks after operation |
| Curses, accuses, is negativistic | |
| "You doctors killed me" | |
| Takes first step, supported on both sides | |
| Brushes his teeth | |

| | |
|---|---|
| *Out of coma* | *October 12* |
| Distressed and tearful about his state and surroundings; "I am dead" | 15 weeks after operation |

Acts very angry, physically violent,
   confused
Laughs
Speaks Arabic to Arab orderlies
Switches to English when told someone
   doesn't know German
Takes off nightshirt
Applies chapstick to his lips
Opens tube of anchovy paste and spreads
   paste on his bread
First home visit: walks upstairs

| | |
|---|---|
| Cooperates in physiotherapy and<br>   occupational therapy<br>Baffled about his mental state;<br>  "I keep saying stupid things"<br>"I want to live"<br>Writes a line<br>Answers telephone<br>Toilet-trained | 16 weeks after operation;<br>1 week after awakening |
| Eats a proper breakfast and a three-course<br>   lunch<br>Opens can of tuna with can opener<br>Uses knife and fork<br>Gets up from toilet unaided<br>Walks with walker | 17 weeks after operation;<br>2 weeks after awakening |
| Makes telephone call from public phone<br>Looks at newspaper<br>Reads letter | 3 weeks after awakening |
| Reads time on analog watch<br>Reads book<br>Works on his dictionary with Rachel<br>Instantly translates German text into English<br>First weekend at home<br>Makes Kiddush (ceremonial blessing<br>   over wine); makes blessing over<br>   loaves and cuts up one of them<br>Remembers exact position of a particular<br>   book in his large library and color of its<br>   cover | 4 weeks after awakening |

Gets out of wheelchair unaided and goes
   to toilet

Laughs at comedy on television            5 weeks after awakening
Makes blessing for reading of the Law
   in synagogue

Goes through his bank statements        6 weeks after awakening

Dresses himself unaided                7 weeks after awakening
Writes a speech for friend's
   seventieth birthday
Writes letters about his illness to his
   friends and relatives

## *Released from hospital*        *November 27*

Reads his mail and articles             8 weeks after awakening
Looks at proofs of his *Haggadah*
Writes down addresses and phone numbers
   of people important to him
Walks up three flights of stairs to attend
   friend's seventieth birthday party;
   delivers speech

Starts going to the day hospital three     9 weeks after awakening
   mornings a week
Stays up late to watch *King Lear* on
   television; is greatly moved by it
Jots down items he needs in his calendar
Writes preface to his *Haggadah*
Reminds me to call doctor for prescription

Makes his own breakfast             10 weeks after awakening
Resumes work on one of his books
Attends his research institute
First social visit
Goes to concert for the first time
Walks with four-pronged cane

Looks up numbers in telephone directory,  12 weeks after awakening
   remembering sequence of alphabet

Memorizes our phone number, our ages,
  and our birthdays

| | |
|---|---|
| Goes alone to synagogue | 14 weeks after awakening |
| Lectures on Bible versions at day hospital | |
| Writes article about his former teacher; it is published in *Ha'aretz* | |

| | |
|---|---|
| Stops going to day hospital | 15 weeks after awakening |
| Goes to the movies | |

| | |
|---|---|
| At Jonathan's wedding dances with bride and gives twenty-minute speech | 29 March 1986; 24 weeks after awakening; |
| Swims | 4 months out of hospital |

| | |
|---|---|
| Gets in and out of bath alone | 5 months out of hospital |
| Walks without cane at home and on campus | |

| | |
|---|---|
| Addresses audience of fifty at Institute for Jewish Studies | 6 months out of hospital |
| Travels alone by bus | |
| Is allowed to take his driving test | |

| | |
|---|---|
| Reads paper at International Congress of Old Testament Studies | 9 months out of hospital |

| | |
|---|---|
| We go to Europe for a month | 10 months out of hospital |

| | |
|---|---|
| Assumes full teaching load at both universities | 11 months out of hospital |

| | |
|---|---|
| Drives own car | 14 months out of hospital |

## Hospitalizations

3 weeks in intensive coronary care
4 weeks in recovery room (intensive care) after operation
6 weeks in cardiac surgery ward
2 weeks in acute geriatric ward
8 weeks in chronic geriatric ward